URBAN FORAGING:

A COOK'S GUIDE TO VANCOUVER... AND BEYOND

Caralyn Campbell
Tracey Shelley-Lavery

Dog Eared Books

Cover illustrations by Wayne Sayer.
Cover designs and chapter illustrations by Bob Krieger.
Photography by Bob Yaremchuk.

Printed in Canada.

Canadian Cataloguing in Publication Data

Campbell, Caralyn & Shelley-Lavery, Tracey
Urban Foraging: A Cook's Guide to Vancouver...And Beyond

ISBN 0-9699061-0-2

1. Food industry and trade - British Columbia - Lower Mainland - Directories. 2. Kitchen utensils industry - British Columbia - Lower Mainland - Directories. 3. Food service - British Columbia - Lower Mainland - Equipment and supplies - Directories. II. Title.

HD9014.C33B75 1994 381'.45664'00257113
C94-900928-8

How do we begin to express our gratitude to the many people who have shared our belief in this book...

To Sandy Hall, Sarah Milroy and Nicola Scott for their chaos control and devotion to the project.

For unfailing emotional sustenance we are eternally grateful to: Bob Krieger, Kelly Elliott, Ollie Baxter-Smith, Norma Shelley, Liz Hart, Kelly Conabree, Jennifer Braidwood, Kim Maloney, Hannah Fisher and Bob Shelley, Cynthia Oliphant, Matt Hill and Jamie Baxter.

For practical advice, panic phone call consolation and assistance above and beyond the call of duty we thank: Brian Lavery, Fontaine Wong, Gillian Shaw, Ann Defeo, Dan Campbell, Leonard McCabe, Arlene Fedoruk, Bill Didur, Bob Yaremchuk, Duncan Fraser, Linda Palmer, Wayne Sayer, Kirk Elliott, Gail Berger, Dorothy Anderson and the staff of Earth's Good Harvest.

For understanding that our hearts were with them: Chelsea and Ryan Campbell, Duncan Shelley, Denise Dobovicnik and Jennifer Munson.

"We love to feel, as we hear appreciative murmurs and smacks of approval, that we have contributed in such a fundamental way to someone else's well-being."

Judith B. Jones

CONTENTS

INTRODUCTION

To live where we do and not feel passionately about food is quite simply -- an incredible shame. As food lovers, there are few more fortunate. We take for granted fresh seafood, abundant local produce and a diverse mix of cultures, each providing us with a unique blend of ingredients and preparation styles. When we need to rest, or celebrate, we have a wonderful array of innovative chefs to feed and inspire us. We are truly blessed. The Pacific Northwest is a food lover's paradise.

Whether you love to cook, or cook because you love to eat, **Urban Foraging** will be a delight for you.

Putting it together has taken us on a whirlwind discovery tour of Vancouver and beyond. We're very excited about the sources we have discovered and the people we have met. If we missed something it was either because we didn't find it or the company didn't provide us with enough information in time for our deadline.

This book is intended to be a guide. The individual sections provide a categorical listing of our sources with a more comprehensive alphabetical directory following. The chapter on Raves and References includes our favourite food literature, restaurants and dream getaways.

We believe our sources and information to be accurate and reliable, but we cannot guarantee any source. All addresses and information were correct up to the date of publication.

As the food industry is a dynamic one, we will update **Urban Foraging** on an annual basis.

If you know of a source for ingredients or equipment that you feel belongs in **Urban Foraging**, please write to us. Our address is on the last page of the book.

Happy feasting!   Caralyn and Tracey.

1

Farm Gate Markets

"When food, in the minds of eaters, is no longer associated with farming and with the land, then the eaters are suffering a kind of cultural amnesia that is misleading and dangerous."

Wendell Berry

ALDOR ACRES
ANDERSON'S POTATOES
ANNIE'S ORCHARD
ASLAN'S ACRE
BARCELONA HAZELNUT PROCESSORS
BELL CREEK FARM
BERRYHAVEN FARM
BERTRAND CREEK FARM
BEST CREEK FARMS
BLUEBERRY HOLLOW
CEDAR COTTAGE FARM
CHERRY JUBILEE
CHERRYHILL FARM
CHILLIWACK RIVER VALLEY NATURAL HONEY
COUNTRY BUMPKINS
DAVE'S ORCHARD
DRIEDIGER FARMS
ELYSIA HERB FARM
FALK FARMS
FORSTBAUER FAMILY NATURAL FOOD FARM
FRANK-LYNN
FRANKE FARMS
FROST HILL FARMS
GREENDALE APPLE FARM
GREENVALE FARMS
HAZELMERE ORGANIC FARMS
HEIRLOOM BEAN COMPANY
HODGINS SMITH
KRAUS BROS
LOWLAND HERB FARM
MAKARA FARMS
MELODIOUS ORCHARD
NINE MILE GARDENS

NORALL ENTERPRISES
PAN'S GARDEN
RALPH'S FARM
RAVENHILL FARM
RED CURRANT FARM
REYNALDA FARMS
ROHAN FARMS
RUN-DOWN WALK-UP FARM
SHELL ROAD FARM
STUBER'S ORCHARD
SUMAS RIVER FARM
THE APPLE FARM
THORNCREST FARM
TWIN OAKS HERB FARM
VAN OOSTEROM BERRIES/ VEGETABLES
WILLOWVIEW FARMS
WINDEMERE NUT GROVE
WISEBEY VEGGIES

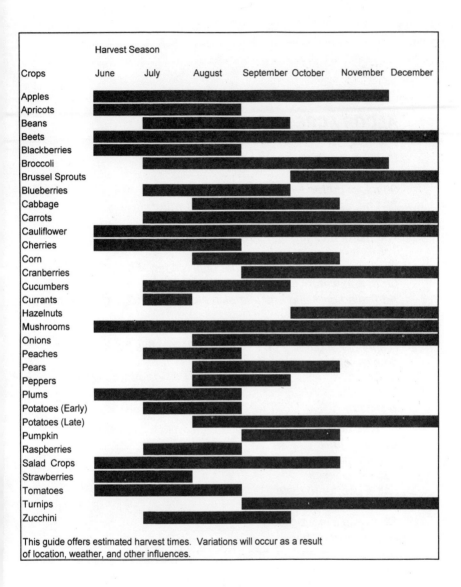

Crops	Harvest Season						
	June	July	August	September	October	November	December
Apples							
Apricots							
Beans							
Beets							
Blackberries							
Broccoli							
Brussel Sprouts							
Blueberries							
Cabbage							
Carrots							
Cauliflower							
Cherries							
Corn							
Cranberries							
Cucumbers							
Currants							
Hazelnuts							
Mushrooms							
Onions							
Peaches							
Pears							
Peppers							
Plums							
Potatoes (Early)							
Potatoes (Late)							
Pumpkin							
Raspberries							
Salad Crops							
Strawberries							
Tomatoes							
Turnips							
Zucchini							

This guide offers estimated harvest times. Variations will occur as a result of location, weather, and other influences.

ALDOR ACRES PUMPKIN SOUP

2 stalks of celery - chopped
1 onion - chopped
30 mL of butter
284 mL can of chicken broth - 2 cans water
150 mL salad dressing
750 mL of mashed or pureed pumpkin

Cook celery and onion in butter until tender. Add soup
broth and water. Simmer for 10 minutes.
Add salad dressing and pumpkin along with salt and
pepper to taste.
Heat and serve.
A sprinkle of parsley on top adds colour to this harvest
time delight.

Aldor Acres

PESTO

500 mL basil (packed)
2 cloves garlic
125 mL pine nuts
125 mL olive oil
salt & pepper to taste

Chop garlic in processor.
Add basil and chop.
Add pine nuts and parmesan and chop.
Add olive oil and blend.
Heat lightly and toss with pasta.

Pan Gardens

2

Markets

*"Bring me berries or such cooling fruit
As the kind, hospitable woods provide."*

Cowper

BARNSTON ISLAND HERB CORPORATION
CHILLIWACK PUBLIC MARKET
CHONG TAI FARM MARKET
DELTA FARM MARKET
GRANVILLE ISLAND PUBLIC MARKET
KIN'S FARM MARKET
LONSDALE QUAY MARKET
MAPLE RIDGE FARM
MARKET AT PARK ROYAL
MARVELLOUS MUSHROOMS
PERESTROIKA PRODUCE
PIKE PLACE
RICHMOND COUNTRY FARMS
RICHMOND PUBLIC MARKET
ROBSON PUBLIC MARKET
SUNSHINE MARKET
WESTMINSTER QUAY PUBLIC MARKET

GOOSEBERRY JAM

*Take about 1.5 kg of gooseberries with 30 mL lemon
juice and chop in blender.*
Add 250 mL water and simmer until soft.
*Mix one package Certo with 1.25 L of berries and bring
to boil in a large kettle.*
Add 5 mL butter and 1.5 L sugar. Boil 1 minute.
Pour into hot, sterile jars. Yields about 2 L.

Thorncrest Farms

GAIL'S BLENDER-FREEZER APPLE SAUCE

Wash, quarter and core apples. Do not peel.
Cut quarters into thirds.
*Place in blender with enough water and lemon juice to
start. Blend until fine.*
Pour into big pot and cook until bubbles like porridge.
Pour into hot, sterilised jars leaving head space.
Put lids on jars and let cool.
Store in freezer.

The Apple Farm

3

Ethnic

"Food is a language that is spoken, one way or another, in every life."

Michael Frank

A BOSA AND COMPANY LTD
ALL INDIA FOODS
AVIV KOSHER MEATS DELI AND BAKERY
BENNY'S BAGELS
BOSS BAKERY AND RESTAURANT LTD
CARMELO PASTRY SHOP
CIOFFI'S MEAT MARKET
DUSSA'S HAM AND CHEESE LTD
ERNIE'S AUSTRIAN BAKERY
ESPRESSO CAPPUCCINO COFFEE CO
EXPRESSOHEAD COFFEE HOUSE
FALCONE BROTHERS' MEAT MARKET
FAZIO FOODS INTERNATIONAL LTD
FUJIYA FISH AND JAPANESE FOODS
GALLOWAYS SPECIALTY FOODS
HALAL MEATS AND DELI
HING LOONG COMPANY
HING WAH LTD
INTERPORT SALES
JB FOODS
JERUSALEM BAKERY/ELMASU MARKET
JOSIE'S SPECIALTY FOODS AND DELI
KAM TONG ENTERPRISES LTD
KOHLER'S EUROPEAN SAUSAGE LTD
LA BAGUETTE ET L'ECHALOTTE
LA CASA GELATO
LOONG FOONG BAKERY
MARIO'S GELATI
MAX'S DELI & BAKERY
MAXIM'S BAKERY AND RESTAURANT
MING WO
MUM'S ITALIAN GELATO
NAZARE BBQ CHICKEN
OLIVIERI FOODS
PARTHENON SUPERMARKET

PATELS
PATISSERIE BORDEAUX
PATISSERIE BRUXELLES INC. (D.C. DUBY)
PERESTROIKA PRODUCE
POLONIA SAUSAGE
QUE PASA
SABRA'S KOSHER BAKERY AND DELI
SHIMIZU SHOTEN
SINGH FOODS
SLAVIC DELICATESSAN
SOLLY'S BAGELRY
SUSHI SHOP
TEN REN TEA & GINSENG COMPANY
THE PATTY SHOP
TORREFAZIONE COLIERA
TOSI ITALIAN FOOD IMPORT COMPANY
UGO AND JOE'S FRESH MEATS AND DELI
VAN CHEONG TEA COMPANY
VENEZIA ICE CREAM
WEST SIDE SPECIALTY FOODS
ZORBA'S BAKERY AND FOODS LTD

4

Seafood

"The silvery fish,
Grazing at large in meadows submarine,
Fresh from the wave now cheers our festive board."
                                    from the Home Cookbook
                                              Toronto, 1889

ANGLER SMOKEHOUSE
FUJIYA FISH AND JAPANESE FOODS
GRAEM CASTELL'S FINEST FOODS
IMPERIAL SALMON HOUSE
KAM TONG ENTERPRISES LTD
LOX ROYALE
SEVEN SEAS FISH COMPANY
SILVA-GLO TROUT FARMS LTD
SILVER BROOK U-CATCH
STEVESTON FISH SHOPPE
STEVESTON PUBLIC FISH SALES FLOAT
SUPERIOR FISH MARKET
THE LOBSTER MAN
VALLEY FRESH FISH

ENRAGED OIL

strips of orange zest - 2 x 1/2"
bay leaves
dried long red chile peppers
whole allspice
black peppercorns
light olive oil
sterilised bottles

Place a strip of orange zest, one bay leaf, one chile pepper, three allspice and six peppercorns in each decorative, clean bottle.
Cover with oil and let steep at least two weeks to bring out the flavours.

Basic Stock

5

Gourmet Take-outs and Meats

"Some hae meat and canna eat,
And some wad eat that want it;
But we hae meat, and we can eat,
And sae the Lord be thankit."

Robbie Burns

ARBUTUS BAY DEER FARMS
ARBUTUS REAL FOOD MARKET
AULD SCOTTISH LARDER
AVIV KOSHER MEATS, DELI AND BAKERY
BREAD GARDEN
CAMPBELL'S PHEASANTRY
CIOFFI'S MEAT MARKET AND DELI
ELIZABETH'S GOURMET DELIGHTS AND CATERING
FALCONE BROTHERS' MEAT MARKET
GRAEM CASTELL'S FINEST FOODS
GRANDMAISON BEEF FARM LTD
HALAL MEATS & DELI
JD FARMS SPECIALTY TURKEY STORE
JACKSON'S MEATS
JOSIE'S SPECIALTY FOODS AND DELI
KAM TONG ENTERPRISES LTD
KERRISDALE MEAT MARKET
KOHLER'S EUROPEAN SAUSAGE LTD
LA TOQUE BLANCHE & GOURMET CATERING
LAZY GOURMET
LESLEY STOWE FINE FOODS
MARINER MEATS LTD
MAX'S DELI & BAKERY
NAZARE BBQ CHICKEN
NOT JUST DESSERTS
ONLY ORIANA
P AND G SAUSAGE LTD
PACE'S GOURMET MEATS
POLONIA SAUSAGE
QUE PASA
QUEEN'S PARK MEAT MARKET
RICHMOND COUNTRY FARMS
RODEAR MEATS
RUN-DOWN WALK-UP FARM
SABRA'S KOSHER BAKERY AND DELI

SLAVIC DELICATESSAN
SPAGNOL'S SUPER MARKET
STOCK MARKET
THE REMARKABLE DOG
UGO AND JOE'S FRESH MEATS AND DELI
VANCOUVER COMMUNITY COLLEGE

6

Baked Goods

"Sing a song of sixpence a pocket full of rye
Four and twenty blackbirds, baked in a pie;
When the pie was opened, the birds began to sing;
Wasn't that a dainty dish to set before a king?"

Anonymous

23

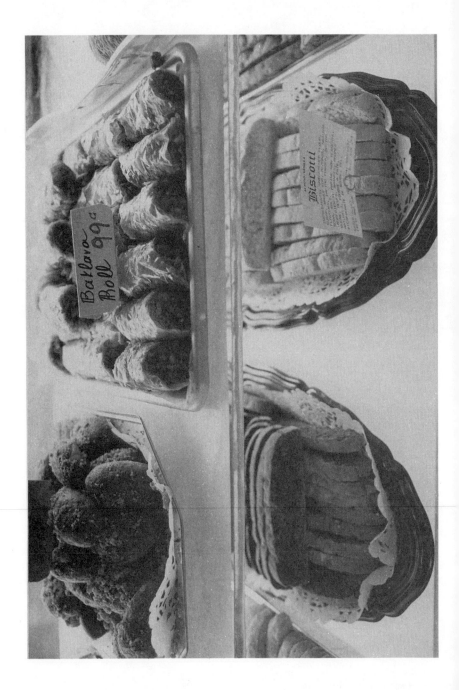

A PIECE OF CAKE
AU CHOCOLAT
AVIV KOSHER MEATS, DELI AND BAKERY
BENNY'S BAGELS
BON TON PASTRY AND CONFECTIONARY
BOSS BAKERY AND RESTAURANT LTD
BREAD GARDEN BAKERY AND CAFE
CAKE OCCASIONS
CARMELO PASTRY SHOP
CHARLIE'S CHOCOLATE FACTORY
ECCO IL PANE
ERNIE'S AUSTRIAN BAKERY
EUROPEAN CHEESECAKE FACTORY
HOUSE OF BRUSSELS CHOCOLATES
JERUSALEM BAKERY/ELMASU MARKET
LA BAGUETTE ET L'ECHALOTTE
LE CHOCOLATE BELGE DANIEL
LE MERIDIEN'S CHOCOLATE BAR
LEE'S CANDIES
LOONG FOONG BAKERY
MAX'S DELI & BAKERY
MAXIM'S BAKERY & RESTAURANT
NOT JUST DESSERTS
PATISSERIE BORDEAUX
PATISSERIE BRUXELLES INC. (D.C. DUBY)
PURDYS
RICHARD'S IMPORTED CANDIES
SABRA'S KOSHER BAKERY AND DELI
SOLLY'S BAGELRY
SWEET OBSESSION
TERRA BREADS
TRENANT PARK BAKERY AND CAFE ·
TRUE CONFECTIONS
UPRISING BAKERY
ZORBA'S BAKERY & FOODS LTD

CHOCOLATE PATE WITH RASPBERRY SAUCE

400 g semi-sweet grated chocolate
250 mL whipping cream
50 g butter
4 egg yolks
200 mL icing sugar

Line 9 x 5 loaf pan with plastic wrap and cover all edges.
Place grated chocolate in a medium bowl with butter
around the edges. Place bowl of chocolate over sauce
pan of simmering water. Scald whipping cream in
another saucepan. Pour cream slowly into chocolate
mixture when butter is half melted. Stir slowly until all of
the cream has been added. Take off heat and whisk
together egg yolks and icing sugar and fold gently into
chocolate mixture. Do not overmix. Pour into loaf pan,
smoothing until even. This will fill loaf pan half way.
Freeze overnight. Remove from freezer and place in
fridge.

Raspberry Sauce (Yields 250 mL)

500 mL raspberries
200 mL sugar
125 mL water
5 mL lemon juice

Put berries in a saucepan. Add water, sugar, lemon.
Bring to a boil. Strain and reduce if thicker consistency
is desired.

Salmon House

26

7

Natural Foods, Organics, Spices, Coffee and Tea

"If we look, food has the structure of linguistics and religion. It is sociology and economics, politics and cultural definition; it is history, memory, and passion interwoven with style as clearly as painting, literature, dance, music and architecture."

Barbara Kafka

AGORA FOOD CO-OP ASSOCIATION
ANITA'S ORGANIC GRAINS
ARBUTUS REAL FOOD MARKET
BREWSTER'S COFFEE
CAPERS WHOLE FOOD MARKET
CHOICES MARKET
CIRCLING DAWN ORGANIC FOODS
CONTINENTAL COFFEE
CROFT'S HEALTH PRODUCTS
CRS WORKERS' CO-OP HORIZON DISTRIBUTION
EARTH'S GOOD HARVEST
ESPRESSO CAPPUCCINO COFFEE MACHINE CO
GAIA GARDEN HERBAL APOTHECARY
GALLOWAYS SPECIALTY FOODS
GLORIOUS GARNISH AND SEASONAL SALAD
HEARTS NATURAL FOOD MARKET
INTERPORT SALES
KITSILANO NATURAL FOOD STORE
LESLEY STOWE FINE FOODS
MURCHIES TEA & COFFEE LTD
PAN'S GARDEN
SOUTH CHINA SEAS TRADING COMPANY
STARBUCKS
SWEET CHERUBIM
TEN REN TEA & GINSENG COMPANY
THE BAKEHOUSE BAKERY DELI CAFE
TORREFAZIONE COLIERA
VAN CHEONG TEA COMPANY
VANCOUVER SPICE COMPANY
WEST SIDE SPECIALTY FOODS
YOKA'S COFFEE AND HONEY

GARLIC SOUP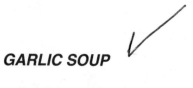

15 ml olive or canola oil
1 bunch green onions, green and white part also,
chopped
1 1/2 heads of garlic (18-22) peeled only
1 bunch celery, diced
2 medium potatoes, peeled and cubed
1.5 L vegetable broth
20 ml coarsely ground pepper
15 ml oregano
2 ml cumin

Saute green onions in oil in a large pot until tender. Add
potatoes, 1 litre only of the vegetable broth and spices.
Simmer 30 minutes or until vegetables are tender.
Remove from heat and puree in a food processor or
blender until smooth, adding reserved vegetable broth to
get the desired consistency.
Serve hot, add salt, pepper and parmesan cheese to
taste.
Serves 6-8.

Choices Market

8

Dairy

"The friendly cow all red and white,
I love with all my heart:
She gives me cream with all her might,
To eat with apple tart."

Robert Louis Stevenson

31

AVALON DAIRY
BIRCHWOOD DAIRY
CHILLIWACK MILK MAID DAIRY LTD
DAYBREAK FARMS
DUSSA'S HAM AND CHEESE LTD
FORSTER'S FINE CHEESE
JERSEY FARM
LA CASA GELATO
LA GROTTA DEL FORMAGGIO
MARIO'S GELATI
MUM'S ITALIAN GELATO
NATIONAL CHEESE COMPANY
VENEZIA ICE CREAM

PEPPER SEARED SALMON ON CORN GRIDDLE CAKES

Salmon fillet
2 mL baking powder
50 mL cornmeal
50 mL all purpose flour
250 mL corn kernels
50 mL milk
15 mL diced red pepper
15 mL diced yellow pepper

5 mL diced jalapeno
45 mL unsalted butter
1 egg
2 egg yolks
1 mL salt
Ground pepper
15 g goat cheese

Combine cornmeal, flour and baking powder. In a food processor puree 125 mL corn kernels until smooth. Place remaining 125 mL kernels and corn puree in a mixing bowl and whisk in milk, diced peppers, jalapeno peppers and conbined dry ingredients.
In a separate bowl whisk together melted butter, eggs and egg yolks. Stir in the corn mixture and season with salt and pepper.
Cook in heavy skillet until golden brown.
Remove skin from salmon and cut 4-6 pieces. Season with lemon and pepper. Sear salmon 20-30 seconds either side and remove from pan.
Serve with goat cheese sprinkled over the top sun-dried tomato vinaigrette

SUN-DRIED TOMATO VINAIGRETTE

30 g sun-dried tomato
2 shallots finely chopped
1 mL chopped garlic
5 mL fresh lemon juice
2 mL ground pepper

45 mL white wine vinegar
50 mL white wine
2 mL salt
5 mL sugar
50 mL plus 30 mL sunflower oil

Soak sun-dried tomato for 1 minute in boiling water. Drain tomato and julienne very fine.
Combine all ingredients and puree in blender 2-3 minutes.

Salmon Month: Chef Deb Connors "Horizons"

9

Co-ops, Wholesalers, Importers & Bulk Goods

*"The man who invites his friends to his table,
and fails to give his personal attention to the meal
they are going to eat, is unworthy to have any friends."*

Jean-Althelme Brillat-Savarin

A BOSA AND COMPANY LTD
AGORA CO-OP FOOD ASSOCIATION
ALL INDIA FOODS
ANITA'S ORGANIC GRAINS
CIRCLING DAWN ORGANIC FOODS
CRS WORKERS' COOP HORIZON DISTRIBUTION
FAMOUS FOODS
FAZIO FOODS INTERNATIONAL LTD
GALLOWAYS SPECIALTY FOODS
GLORIOUS GARNISH AND SEASONAL SALAD
INTERPORT SALES
JB FOODS
JERUSALEM BAKERY/ELMASU MARKET
LOX ROYALE
MARINER MEATS LTD
NATIONAL CHEESE COMPANY
OLIVIERI FOODS
ONLY ORIANA
PARTHENON SUPERMARKET
PATELS
SWEET CHERUBIM
TOSI ITALIAN FOOD IMPORT COMPANY
UPRISING BAKERY

BLUEBERRY SALSA

1/2 Large pink grapefruit
2 tbsp Spanish Onion (finely diced)
1 Jalapeno pepper (finely diced)
1 tsp Honey
1 tbsp Fresh squeezed lime juice
1 cup Blueberries (fresh or frozen)
2 tbsp Cilantro (finely chopped)

Method
Section pink grapefruit and discard membrane. Dice
grapefruit and mix with other salsa ingredients. Spoon
salsa over salmon or other West Coast delicacies.

Terry Multhauf - Joe Fortes
(Salmon Month)

10

Spirits

"Water is for quenching the thirst. Wine, according to its quality and the soil where it was grown, is a necessary tonic, a luxury, and a fitting tribute to good food."

Colette

A BOSA AND COMPANY LTD
CAMBIE STREET LIQUOR STORE
DIVINO'S QUAYSIDE WINE CELLAR
DOMAINE DE CHABERTON ESTATE WINERY
LIBERTY WINE MERCHANT
MARK ANTHONY WINE MART
MARQUIS WINE CELLAR
RENAISSANCE WINE MERCHANTS
SPAGNOL'S WINE AND BEER MAKING SUPPLIES
VINTAGE CONSULTANTS

ROAST MUSSELS WITH GINGER

1/4 bunch cilantro, chopped
skinned and diced ginger root
1 ounce olive oil
1 ounce rehydrated and chopped sun-dried tomatoes
3 lbs fresh mussels, rinsed and beards removed
1 ounce minced garlic
4 tbsp. white wine
juice from 1/2 lemon

Heat ovenproof pan with olive oil until very hot and add
all remaining ingredients except wine and lemon juice.
Toss a couple of times and place in oven at 400F.
Cooking time is approximately 5-10 minutes. Mussels
will open when cooked.
Remove from oven when cooked and place pan on
burner. Add wine and lemon juice.
Serve immediately.

BC Wine Country

11

Cookware

"I found a home where my father's storm could be tamed to the bubbles and steam of my grandmother's samovar."

Barbara Kafka

43

ARMY AND NAVY
ATKINSON'S
BASIC STOCK
BON CHEF KITCHEN
CASA
CASSIDY'S
CHOCOLATE MOUSSE KITCHENWARE
COOKSHOP
DRINKWATER AND COMPANY FINE COOKWARE
DUNLEVY SALES
ECHO'S DISCONTINUED CHINA AND SILVER
ESPRESSO CAPPUCCINO COFFEE MACHINE CO
FRASER VALLEY SALADMASTER
HOUSE OF KNIVES
ITALCANA IMPORTERS
KITCHEN SHELF
MARKET KITCHEN
MING WO
PARAGON FOOD EQUIPMENT
PUDDIFOOTS
RAVENSBERGEN BAKERY SUPPLIES
RUSSELL FOOD EQUIPMENT
SUR LA TABLE
TOOLS AND TECHNIQUES
TRAIL APPLIANCES

CHOCOLATE

Chocolate is the food substance made of cocoa, sugar, and sometimes to a lesser extent: milk, nuts, honey, and dried fruits. Chocolate's history dates back to the Aztecs, who drank "Xocoatl" to celebrate gods and enjoy its aphrodisiac qualities. Later, chocolate was said to be capable of curing everything from insomnia to weight gain and loss. Today there are still many theories about chocolate's unique abilities...but to the true chocolate lover one thing remains the same; a good chocolate is a taste experience to be savoured. Chocolate's quality can be judged by its shininess, freedom from lumps, bubbles and white specks, its ability to melt on the tongue like butter but not leave a waxy residue on the roof of the mouth, and aroma of chocolate as opposed to cocoa.

The basic chocolate types include:
unsweetened or baking chocolate, semi-sweet or bitter-sweet chocolate, cocoa powder, milk chocolate, white chocolate, and couverture or coating chocolate.

Unsweetened: pure chocolate with no sugar added
Semisweet: chocolate product using not less than 35 per cent cocoa
Cocoa powder: there are three types of cocoa powders including
unsweetened, Dutch processed(treated with alkali) and drinking chocolate powder(watch for high sugar content and flour additives)
Milk chocolate: contains not less than 10 per cent pure chocolate
White chocolate: not a true chocolate, but is does contain cocoa butter
Couverture: a coating used by candy makers, no pure chocolate

12

Raves and References

*"Individuals predestined to gourmandism are generally of
medium height; they have round or square faces, bright eyes,
small foreheads, short noses, full lips, and well-rounded chins.
The women are buxom pretty rather than beautiful, with a
tendency to run to fat...Such is the exterior beneath which to
look for the most agreeable company, for these are the guests
who accept everything they are offered, eat slowly, and
savour each morsel thoughtfully. They are never in a hurry to
leave the place where they have found true hospitality; and
they are invited to stay all evening because they know the
games and pastimes appropriate to gastronomical gatherings.
Those, on the contrary, to whom Nature has refused an
aptitude for the pleasures of taste, have long faces, noses,
and eyes; whatever their height, there is something elongated
in their proportions. Their hair is dark and flat, and they are
never plump; it was they who invented trousers."*

Jean-Althelme Brillat-Savarin

ALIVE MAGAZINE
ALPINE WINE FESTIVAL
AMBROSIA
BC OKANAGAN WINE FESTIVAL
BC WINE COUNTRY
BC WINE INSTITUTE
BC WINE TRAILS
BALLYMALOE COOKERY SCHOOL
BANFF SPRINGS FESTIVAL
BISHOP'S
BLACKBERRY BOOKS
BON APPETIT
BOOK WAREHOUSE
BREAKFAST IN BED
BREWMASTER'S FESTIVAL
CANADIAN ORGANIC ADVISORY COUNCIL
CAPRIAL'S SEASONAL KITCHEN
CERTIFIED ORGANIC ASSOCIATION
CHOCOLATIER
CITY FOOD MAGAZINE
COMMUNITY SHARED AGRICULTURAL ORG
COOKSHOP COOKING SCHOOL
CSA RESOURCE CENTRE
DIAL-A-DIETITIAN
DUBRULLE FRENCH CULINARY SCHOOL
DUTHIE'S BOOK STORE
ECOLE DE GASTRONOMIE FRANCAISE
ELIZABETH'S GOURMET DELIGHTS AND CATERING
FARM FOLK/CITY FOLK
FARM FRESH GUIDE
FAST & FANTASTIC
FIVE STAR FOOD
FRASER VALLEY FARM FRESH GUIDE
FROM A COASTAL KITCHEN
GIRAFFE RESTAURANT

GOURMET MAGAZINE
GRANVILLE ISLAND MARKET COOKBOOK
GRAPE EXPECTATIONS
GREAT CHEFS AT MONDAVI WINERY
GREAT CULINARY ADVENTURES
GREAT WOK CHINESE RESTAURANT
GROCER TODAY
HARVEST GUIDE
HASTINGS HOUSE
HOSTELLERIE DE CRILLON LE BRAVE
INTERNATIONAL WINE FESTIVAL
JURGEN GOTHE
KITCHEN SHELF
LA BELLE AUBERGE
LA TOQUE BLANCHE
LA VARENNE SUMMER SCHOOL
LE CORDON BLEU
LE CORDON BLEU PARIS COOK SCHOOL
LE MANOIR AUX QUAT-SAISONS
LE MERIDIEN CHOCOLATE BAR
LIGHTHEARTED COOKING
MARCELLA & VICTOR HAZAN
MARKET KITCHEN
MOOSEWOOD COOKBOOK
MY THAI RESTAURANT
NORTHWEST PALATE
OKANAGAN WINE FESTIVAL
PACIFIC NORTHWEST
PAPI'S
PINK PEPPERCORN BOOKSTORE

RUBINA TANDOORI LAZEEZ CUISINE
SALMON HOUSE ON THE HILL
SALMON MONTH
SALSA, SAMBAS, CHUTNEYS & CHOW CHOWS
SANTA FE CAFE
SILVER PALATE COOKBOOK
SONOMA WINE TOUR
SOOKE HARBOUR HOUSE
SOUTH CHINA SEAS TRADING COMPANY
STAR ANISE
TASTE OF THE NATION
THAI COOKING SCHOOL
THE NEW BASICS COOKBOOK
THE PROVINCE
THE URBAN GARDENER
THE VANCOUVER SUN
THE VILLAGE BAKER
UMBERTO'S PASTA BOOK
VANCOUVER MAGAZINE
VARI BERRY FRUIT DISTRIBUTORS
VILLA DELIA TUSCANY COOKING SCHOOL
WESTERN LIVING MAGAZINE
WINE TIDINGS
WINE AND DINE
YELLOW POINT LODGE

BLUEBERRY CHEESECAKE WITH BLUEBERRY TOPPING

CRUST
1 cup graham cracker crumbs
1/4 cup unsalted butter
1 tablespoon sugar

FILLING
4 x 8 ounce packages cream cheese - room temperature
1 cup sugar
2 tablespoons fresh lemon juice
1 tablespoon vanilla extract
1 1/2 teaspoons grated lemon peel
4 large eggs
1 cup blueberries
1 tablespoon all purpose flour

TOPPING
1 1/2 cups blueberries
1/4 cup sugar
1 1/2 teaspoons cornstarch

FOR CRUST: Preheat oven to 375F. Mix all ingredients in bowl. Press mixture onto bottom (not sides) of 9" springform pan with 2 3/4" sides.

FOR FILLING: Beat cream cheese, sugar, lemon juice, vanilla and lemon peel in large bowl until smooth. Add eggs one at a time, beating just until combined. Toss blueberries with flour. Stir into cream cheese mixture. Pour filling into crust. Bake until eggs are set but centre still moves slightly when cake is shaken - about one hour. Refrigerate overnight.

FOR TOPPING: Stir one cup berries, sugar and cornstarch in heavy medium saucepan over medium heat until sugar dissolves. Increase heat and boil until juices are thick and clear, stirring occasionally, about three minutes. Mix in remaining 1/2 cup blueberries. Cool topping completely.
Pour topping over cheesecake. Refrigerate until topping sets, about two hours. Release pan sides from cake. Cut into slices and serve.

Elizabeth's Gourmet Delights as printed in "Bon Appetit"

DIRECTORY OF SOURCES

A - Z

A

A BOSA AND COMPANY LTD
562 VICTORIA DRIVE, VANCOUVER
PHONE: 253-5578   FAX: 253-5656
HOURS: Mon-Thurs 8:30-5:30, Sat-Sun 8:30-8

Imported fine foods from many countries including Italy,
Spain and Portugal. Grapes and juice for winemaking,
from California. The company specializes in olive oil,
vinegars, pastas, cheeses, cured meats, coffee and
condiments.
Family-operated business for more than 35 years,
offering quality products at affordable prices, with an
emphasis on personalized, friendly service.
Bulk items and quantity discounts are available.

A PIECE OF CAKE
3790 WEST 10TH AVENUE, VANCOUVER
PHONE: 228-9816
HOURS: Mon-Fri 7-12, Sat 8:30-12
          Sun 9-10

Excellent coffee, muffins, tea biscuits, strudel, sticky
buns, cakes by the slice, birthday and wedding cakes,
special occasion cakes. Baking done on premises from
scratch. No preservatives or stabilizers used. Fresh
homemade lunches also served. Reasonable prices.
Friendly family-run store. The chocolate pecan cake is
incredible. Wholesale price list available. Established in
1981 as the first espresso bar and bakery on the west
side of Vancouver.

AGORA CO-OP FOOD ASSOCIATION
3420 WEST BROADWAY, VANCOUVER
PHONE: 733-3505   FAX: 731-5497
HOURS: Mon-Fri 12-7, Sat-Sun 11-6

Organic produce and health food products. Community
based non-profit co-operative. Some local products.
Large volume discounts available. Members can order
case lots at cost plus 15 per cent (lifetime membership
is $75 per family).
Eighteen years on the west side in Vancouver.

ALDOR ACRES
24990-84TH AVENUE, LANGLEY
PHONE: 530-0704   FAX: 530-0860
HOURS: Month of October only

A GIANT PUMPKIN PATCH. Pumpkins and some end
of fall crops while quantities last. ALDOR ACRES caters
to schools and families during October with a farm
animal display and petting area.

ALIVE MAGAZINE
SIEGFRIED GURSCHE EDITOR-IN-CHIEF
7436 FRASER PARK DRIVE, BURNABY

Health and nutrition journal. Published 11 times a year.

ALL INDIA FOODS
6517 MAIN STREET, VANCOUVER
PHONE: 324-1686

One of the largest stocks of Indian specialty foods and
seasonings in North America. This spacious store
features many varieties of spices, curry powders,
chutneys, and chilies. Bulk food, fresh produce, and
inexpensive milk are also available here.

ALPINE WINE FESTIVAL
PHONE: 685-1007 or 932-3434

Call for details about the 1995 event.

AMBROSIA
COOKING SCHOOL: MAUREEN GOULET
3985 BAYRIDGE AVENUE, WEST VANCOUVER
PHONE: 922-6644   FAX : 922-6694

Goulet's classes feature guest chefs such as Wolfgang
Von Weiser/Four Seasons, Ernst Dorfler/Pan Pacific,
Adam Busby/Star Anise and many more. She offers
classes in her home as well as at the Chateau Whistler
and the Empress Hotel in Victoria. These are weekend
getaway cooking classes. All classes include wine from
local importers, recipes of the dishes prepared as well
as the privilege of eating fine food.
Goulet has been in business for 12 years.

ANDERSON'S POTATOES

33625 TOWNSHIPLINE ROAD, MATSQUI
PHONE: 852-3244   FAX: 852-1957
HOURS: September-March: Daily 7-7

ANDERSON'S has been selling Burbank Russet (also
known as Netted Gem), Yukon Gold, Red Norland and
Pontiac potatoes for 40 years, with a commitment to
quality that has afforded them a second generation of
loyal customers from Masset to Calgary. Large volume
discount available.
Drop by this four-generation farm, for fine potatoes and
great stories.

ANGLER SMOKEHOUSE

8030 GRANVILLE, VANCOUVER
PHONE: 266-9019   FAX: 266-1039

The ANGLER offers cold-smoked Sockeye, Coho,
Spring and Steelhead. They also custom-smoke "wild"
Pacific salmon to make lox or smoked salmon. The
product is packaged in a heat-processed, vacuum-
treated foil pack that needs no refrigeration. The
ANGLER will also ship smoked fish anywhere in the
world.

ANITA'S ORGANIC GRAINS
5450 TESKEY ROAD, SARDIS
PHONE: 858-8199
HOURS: Tues-Fri 9-6, Sat 9-5

Wheat and rye kernels, fresh stone-ground whole wheat
and rye flour, unbleached white flour, fresh homestyle
bread, multi-grain pancake and waffle mix. All products
are made with fresh certified organic stone-ground flour.
Whole wheat and rye flours are stone-ground daily.
Also sells rolled oats, seven-grain cereal, kamut and
spelt. Price will vary depending on quantity. The grain
used is grown on a certified organic farm in
Saskatchewan.
ANITA'S delivers fresh stone-ground flour and pancake
mix to Capers bakeries and stores in West Vancouver
and Kitsilano. For large orders ($20 or more)
arrangements can be made to meet the truck.

ANNIE'S ORCHARD
4092 248TH STREET, ALDERGROVE
PHONE: 856-3041
HOURS: August-November: Mon-Sat 8-8, Sun

Sells approximately 50 varieties of fresh-picked apples.
This family-operated business uses Integrated Pest
Management.

ARBUTUS BAY DEER FARMS
777 BEECHWOOD DRIVE, MAYNE ISLAND
PHONE/FAX: 539-2301

Through ORDERS ONLY. Ask for price list.
Produces mouth-watering gourmet foods made from
Fenison, their trademark for farmed fallow venison. The
deer are organically raised. Will ship their products.
Vacuum packed. Low fat content. Products: fenison pate
preserved in cognac; stroganoff; and medallions of
fenison in black currant and red wine. Venison has one-
sixth the cholesterol, one-fifth the fat, and one-third the
calories of beef or pork. The company also sells a wide
range of deerskin clothing products.

ARBUTUS REAL FOOD MARKET
2200 ARBUTUS STREET, VANCOUVER
PHONE: 736-5644   FAX: 738-8354
HOURS: Mon-Fri 8-8, Sat 8:30-8
            Sun 10-7

Healthy, inexpensive gourmet foods and fresh bakery
items. Soon will include deli, espresso, and fresh juices.
ARBUTUS MARKET has that old-fashioned country-
store charm. Local artists' works are on display. Unique
spices such as Galangal powder, achiote, tamarind and
vanilla sugar. Gourmet take-out includes veggie rolls,
spinach pizza, bird's nest cookies. Will special order for
items, especially those in the health food line.

ARMY AND NAVY
27 WEST HASTINGS, VANCOUVER
PHONE: 682-6644   FAX: 682-2026
HOURS: Mon-Wed 9-5:30, Thu 9-9, Sat 9-5:30
        Sun 11-5

A great place to scour around for a wide assortment of
kitchen essentials. Occasionally you'll find tremendous
bargains on quality cookware.

ASLAN'S ACRE
46985 BAILEY ROAD RR#2, SARDIS
PHONE: 858-3631
HOURS: May-December: Mon-Sat 8-6

This small farm offers seasonal produce, selling
boysenberries, tayberries, and rhubarb early in the
summer, Super Sweet table corn in August, and apples
in the fall. Apple varieties include Sunrise, Royal Gala,
Elstar, Jonagold, Fuji, Golden Delicious, Cox Orange,
and Northern Spy.

ATKINSON'S
3057 GRANVILLE, VANCOUVER
PHONE: 736-3378
HOURS: Tues-Sat 10-5:30

This South Granville store specializes in high-end
European linens, silver, china and crystal. Also offers
French crystal, Pratesi Egyptian cotton table linens, and
Italian damask placemats, tablecloths, and napkins. In
business for 10 years, the owner has opened a second
store down the street at Granville and 8th Avenue,
which features the more familiar dinnerware lines.

61

AULD SCOTTISH LARDER
4022 HASTINGS STREET, BURNABY
PHONE: 294-6616
HOURS: Mon-Sat 9-6

Specializes in food imports from the United Kingdom, additive and preservative-free products and their own smoked products. There is an in-store smokehouse and in-store bakery. Everything, except imports, is made on the premises. They offer Ayrshire bacon, Ayrshire ham, black pudding, scones, oatcakes, white pudding, haggis, scotch pies, bridies, Aberdeen Rowies, steak pies, Scotch eggs, Lorne sausage, Scotch bread, empires. Please phone for details about large volume discounts.

AVALON DAIRY
5805 WALES, VANCOUVER
PHONE: 434-2434
HOURS: Mon-Fri 8:30-5:30, Sat 9-5

Products include cow's milk, cheese, ice cream, yoghurt, butter, cereal, whipped cream and goat's milk. Will deliver through independent drivers. Retail outlet on the premises.

AVIV KOSHER MEATS DELI AND BAKERY
3710 OAK STREET
PHONE: 736-5888
HOURS: Mon-Thu 8:30-6:30, Fri 7-3, Sun 8:30-4

Breads (try their New York rye), baked goods (delicious twisted poppy seed bagels) and deli products are available at this friendly store. Also available is a good selection of imported kosher products, yoghurt cheese, as well as refrigerated drinks. Their pastrami is superb.

AU CHOCOLAT
1702 DAVIE, VANCOUVER
PHONE: 682-3536

Specializes in chocolate truffles, decadent cheesecakes (with names like white chocolate almond, and double chocolate hazelnut), and other chocolate sweets and desserts. Fresh ice creams are made on site in the summer.

B

BC OKANAGAN WINE FESTIVAL
185 LAKESHORE DRIVE, PENTICTON
PHONE: 490-8866   FAX: 492-611
Call for details about the 1995 festival.

BC WINE COUNTRY
KAREN AND LARRY WIDMER
BOX 24021, KELOWNA
1-800-667-3848

An informative and entertaining quarterly wine
magazine. Includes recipes and reviews, as well as a
directory of BC wine producers.

BC WINE INSTITUTE
5 1864 SPALL ROAD, KELOWNA
PHONE: 1-800-661-2294

Write or call the institute with your questions about wine.

BC WINE TRAILS
DAVE GAMBLE
BOX 1077, SUMMERLAND
PHONE: 494-7733   FAX: 494 7737

A community-newspaper style quarterly. Wine buying
information, festival calendars and reviews. Very
informative.

BALLYMALOE COOKERY SCHOOL
KINOITH, SHANAGARRY, COUNTY CORK
IRELAND
PHONE: 011-353-21-646785   FAX: 011-353-21-646909

BANFF SPRINGS CLASSIC
WINE & FOOD FESTIVAL
BOX 960, BANFF, ALBERTA
PHONE: 403-762-6826   FAX: 403-762-8405

Call for details about the 1995 festival.

BARCELONA HAZELNUT PROCESSORS
BOX 319 6682 LOUGHEED HWY, AGASSIZ
PHONE: 796-2555
HOURS: Daily 9-Dark

Ron Wigand offers hazelnuts either in-shell, shelled,
roasted, chopped, ground, pasted, or chocolate covered.
The many products are ideal for snacks, cooking,
baking, or as gifts. Mail orders and pre-orders are
available. Tours of the farm are given with notice.

BARNSTON ISLAND HERBS
R R 17 BARNSTON ISLAND, SURREY
PHONE: 581-8017   FAX: 581-0515
HOURS: Mon-Fri 8-5 all year round

Live herbs, fresh cut herbs, baby lettuces, salad mix,
baby vegetables, edible flowers. Consistent supply of
high-quality products. Located on Barnston Island in the

Fraser River. Business was originally started in 1979 and is one of the oldest suppliers of fresh herbs to Lower Mainland hotels and restaurants. Products are only available through various retail outlets in the Lower Mainland. These growers use biological pest control through predator bugs.

BASIC STOCK
2294 W 4TH, VANCOUVER
PHONE: 736-1412
HOURS: Mon-Thu, Sat 9:30-6, Fri 9:30-9, Sun 11-5

Cookware, kitchenware, and 46 varieties of teas and coffees. BASIC STOCK also sells coffeemakers and cappucino machines, stainless steel cook and tableware, and French Pillivuyt bakeware. A great place to browse.

BELL CREEK FARM
10710 BELL ROAD, CHILLIWACK
PHONE: 792-3451
HOURS: Mid June-Mid July: Daily 8-6

Raspberries, gooseberries, red currants and pumpkins. Located on Fairfield Island which, according to the farm's owners has the "best soil for growing fruit." School tours are available in the fall. These include a hayride to the patch, a demonstration of pumpkin carving, choice of pumpkin plus mini-pumpkins, a snack, colouring book and stickers. Cost is $2.50 per child.

BENNY'S BAGELS
2305 WEST BROADWAY, VANCOUVER
PHONE: 736-4686
HOURS: Daily 24 hours

There's more to BENNY'S than just bagels, but if that's what you need they offer everything from cinnamon/apple/raisin to poppyseed to onion. Try the Sweet Bea bagel if a dessert or morning treat is what you're after: made with sugary dough and filled with coconut, they're a perfect snack when toasted. For a savory meal order the Squealer with the works, and get ready for a spicy Serbian sausage wrapped in bagel dough and topped with a pepper salsa.

BERRYHAVEN FARM
320 MT LEHMAN ROAD SOUTH, ABBOTSFORD
PHONE: 859-6380   FAX: 859-1634
HOURS: July-October: Daily 8-5

This farm produces five varieties of summer raspberries, three types of blackberries, and Heritage fall raspberries. Please call ahead as the operators are usually out in the field.

BERTRAND CREEK FARMS/COLUMBIA VALLEY CLASSICS

1385 FROST ROAD COLUMBIA VALLEY, LINDELL
BEACH
BOX 159
PHONE: 858-5318   FAX: 858-5233
HOURS: Summer-Christmas: Daily 8-5

This farm grows raspberries, blueberries and thornless
blackberries and has had great success with the less
common varieties such as Saskatoons and
gooseberries. They are particularly proud of their black,
white and red currants not usually grown in this area.
Located on the hillside overlooking Cultus Lake, this is
the only Western Canadian fruit farm with an on-
premise, Agriculture Canada-licensed, processing
facility. In this small, well-equipped facility, only the
highest quality berries are used to produce a select line
of jams, jellies and syrups which are sold in "The
Jammy House" gift store. Farm tours and plant tours
are available and can be booked in advance.
Discounts on case sales and large fruit orders are
available.

BEST CREEK FARMS

22625 38TH AVENUE, LANGLEY
PHONE: 530-4376   FAX: 530-4367
HOURS: Daily 10-6

This currant farm has been in operation for five years,
combined with a hobby farm operation. Customers
often remark on the care of the farm and the pleasant

pastoral setting. This is the largest red currant farm within the Vancouver area and is easily accessible. Service is friendly and depending on volume (with some advance notice) discounts are available on larger quantities.

BIRCHWOOD DAIRY
1154 FADDEN ROAD, RR#2, ABBOTSFORD
PHONE: 857-1315   FAX: 857-1315
HOURS: Mon-Sat 9-5:30

Family-operated farm that specializes in farm fresh milk, old fashioned ice cream, frozen yoghurt and feta cheese.

BISHOP'S
2183 WEST 4TH AVENUE, VANCOUVER
PHONE: 738-2025
HOURS: Lunch: Mon-Fri 11:30- 2:30
            Dinner: Mon-Sat 5:30 - 11
                    Sun 5:30 - 10

BISHOP'S use of Northwest foods, and it's superb service make it one of the most highly rated restaurants in Vancouver.

BLACKBERRY BOOKS
1663 DURANLEAU, GRANVILLE ISLAND
PHONE: 685 6188 OR 685 4113
HOURS: Daily 9-9

Good selection of cooking and food-related books.
Check phone book for other locations.

BLUEBERRY HOLLOW
42180 SOUTH SUMAS ROAD, SARDIS
PHONE: 823-6973
HOURS: July 1-August 15: Mon-Sat 9-7
             By appointment in October

One of the original blueberry farms in the area, owners
Ian and Pat Hagemoen offer 12 varieties of berries for
picking during the mid-summer weeks. This farm caters
mainly to the U-pick crowd, but if that's inconvenient,
phone ahead to place an order. In October walnuts and
hazelnuts are ready for harvest.

BON APPETIT
6300 WILSHIRE BOULEVARD, LOS ANGELES,
CALIFORNIA, 90048

A monthly publication loaded with the best recipes from
sources the world over.

BON CHEF KITCHEN STORE
6339 200TH STREET, LANGLEY
PHONE: 532-7993   FAX: 532-7668
HOURS: Mon-Thu, Sat 9-5:30, Fri 9-9, Sun 12-5

BON CHEF is a specialty retailer of moderately-priced
housewares. With more than 2,000 square feet of
space, the store carries a full selection of stainless steel
cookware, cast iron cookware, bakeware, cooking
accessories, kitchen gadgets, knives, woodenware,
kitchen ceramics, and kitchen textiles. It carries a large
selection of mixing bowls and salt and pepper mills as
well. BON CHEF is an authorized Kenwood dealer,
carrying a full line of Kenwood products and
accessories.

BON TON
874 GRANVILLE, VANCOUVER
PHONE: 681-3058
HOURS: Tue-Sat 9:30-6

This pastry shop has been a fixture in Vancouver's
dessert world since the thirties. More than 40 delicately
sweet pastries are still made and sold by this family
owned and operated bakery, with specialties including
marzipan animals, chocolate eclairs, and Diplomat cake.
Don't miss out on the celebrated "Canadian Cheeses,"
two rounds of meringue sandwiching a buttercream
centre, the appearance of which suggests great rounds
of cheddar.

BOOK WAREHOUSE

632 W. BROADWAY, VANCOUVER
PHONE: 873-0661   FAX: 876-5711
HOURS: Daily 10-10

Great prices on a variety of food related books.

THE BOSS BAKERY AND RESTAURANT

1532-534 MAIN STREET, VANCOUVER
PHONE: 683-3860   FAX: 688-2677
HOURS: Daily 7-8

THE BOSS is a Hong Kong-styled bakery and
restaurant. Its unique pastries, Chinese buns, and
elegantly decorated cakes for all occasions have made
it one of the most popular spots in Vancouver. The
restaurant specializes in fried noodles and fried rice.
The food is high quality, the service friendly and the
environment comfortable. The bakery produces
elegantly decorated and tasteful whipping cream cakes
for birthdays, weddings and other occasions. For large
and regular orders, a 20 per cent discount will be
considered.

BREAD GARDEN BAKERY AND CAFE
1880 WEST 1ST, VANCOUVER
PHONE: 738-6684
HOURS: 24 Hours

The BREAD GARDEN has foods and meals to suit
every mood. Special baked goods include their Levain
bread, made without yeast and with a good chewy crust
and their highly acclaimed sourdough. Locals also know
that the bread pudding is the best in the city. Several
locations.

BREAKFAST IN BED
CAROL FREIBERG
SASQUATCH BOOKS, 1990

If you want to create the perfect weekend breakfast,
then this is your book. Recipes are a compilation of
offerings from Bed & Breakfasts throughout the Pacific
Northwest.

BREWMASTER'S FESTIVAL

For details of the 1995 festival, phone 736-4431.

BREWSTER'S COFFEE
2414 MARINE, WEST VANCOUVER
PHONE: 925-9820
HOURS: Mon-Fri 6:30-11, Sat 7-11
        Sun/Holidays 7-10

This coffee house offers a custom roaster (off-site) and
12 blends of coffee. The New York Times is delivered

daily, among other mags and rags, and the umbrella-protected seating beckons customers outside on balmier days.

C

CAKE OCCASIONS
4385 DUNBAR, VANCOUVER
PHONE: 228-9565
HOURS: Tues-Sat 7:30-5:30

Specializes in rolled fondant wedding cakes and custom designed cakes. Customers rave about their multi-grain bread (weighing more than two pounds per loaf). The whole wheat bagels, scones and dessert squares are also a specialty. Wholesome soup-and-sandwich lunches are served in the small restaurant.
Baked goods sell quickly so come early or phone ahead to reserve.
NOTE: Wholesalers are requested to order small quantities.

CAMBIE STREET LIQUOR STORE
5555 CAMBIE, VANCOUVER
PHONE: 266-1321

The CAMBIE STREET LIQUOR STORE carries one of
the finest selections of specialty wines and spirits in the
Lower Mainland.

CAMPBELL'S PHEASANTRY
1991 7902 SATCHELL, MT LEHMAN
PHONE: 856-4375

Free-range pheasant, fresh in season, frozen all year.
Whole birds or cut up.

CANADIAN ORGANIC ADVISORY COUNCIL
CONTACT: CHRISTOPH ALTEMUELLER
RR3 4895 MARSHALL, DUNCAN
PHONE: 746-4117   FAX: 748-4287

CAPERS WHOLE FOOD MARKET
2285 W 4TH AVENUE, VANCOUVER
PHONE: 739-6676   FAX: 739-6640
HOURS: Daily 8-10

Whole food groceries, in-store bakery, organic produce,
organic beef and fish, deli and free-range poultry.
Emphasis on natural and organic products.

CAPERS West Vancouver, 2496 Marine Drive. Open
Monday to Wednesday and Weekends, 7am to 7pm
Thursday and Friday til 9pm.

CAPRIAL'S SEASONAL KITCHEN
CAPRIAL PENCE
ALASKA NORTHWEST BOOKS, WASH, 1991

The recipient of the 1991 James Beard Award for Best
Northwest Chef, Caprial Pence makes full use of fresh
local ingredients in her innovative, yet straightforward
recipes. Her love of the Pacific Northwest is apparent in
this inspiring book.

CARMELO PASTRY SHOP
1399 COMMERCIAL, VANCOUVER
PHONE: 254-7024
HOURS: Mon-Sat 9-5

Italian baking and pastries. Customers rave about the
Tiramisu. Also makes Saint Honore cakes and offers
large volume discounts for weddings, catered events.
Has been in operation for 10 years.

CASA
420 HOWE, VANCOUVER
PHONE: 681-5884
HOURS: Mon-Wed, Sat 9:30-6
          Thu-Fri 9:30-9, Sun 11-6

High quality and reasonably priced, CASA offers home and entertainment ware for every occasion. Items such as hand-painted gift boxes, Portugese pewter and reproduction Ming Dynasty plates sold here, and all goods come with an unconditional money-back refund or exchange.

CASSIDY'S
2323 QUEBEC STREET, VANCOUVER
PHONE: 879-6311   FAX: 879-6337
HOURS: Mon-Fri 8:30-5

Specializes in equipment, china, glassware, smallwares, consulting and design. Large selection and personalized service. Custom fabrication. Discounts available on case lots of glass and installations of china.
CASSIDY'S is a national food service company with 18 outlets.

CEDAR COTTAGE FARM AND NURSERY
640 240TH SREET, LANGLEY
PHONE: 530-1217   FAX: 530-1217
          Please phone first to place order

Main crop: Black and red currants, 3rd week of June to July 15th. Also selling Rhododendrons (spring and early fall), cut holly early December and apples September and October.

The farmhouse, which has been fully restored, was built in 1910. During the 1930's the house was owned by a performer in Buffalo Bill's Wild West Show. The fireplace still has his spurs and horse bit embedded in it.

CERTIFIED ORGANIC ASSOCIATION OF BC
CONTACT: HANS BUCHLER
RR2 S53 COMP6, OLIVER
PHONE: 498-2786

CHARLIE'S CHOCOLATE FACTORY
3746 CANADA WAY, BURNABY
PHONE: 437-8221   FAX: 437-8222
HOURS: Mon-Fri 9-5:30, Sat 9-5

Special molded chocolate made with Callebaut chocolate from Belgium - more than 300 different items. Best quality products at affordable prices. Variety, boxes, cups, chocolates. The store features numerous types of packaging supplies, candy and chocolate-making items that are difficult to find. Large volume discounts available. Warehouse and shop (limited hours) at 1770 McLean Avenue in Port Coquitlam. Best selection, assortments and varieties at 3746 Canada Way in Burnaby.

CHERRY JUBILEE
2017 272ND STREET, ALDERGROVE
PHONE: 856-5844
HOURS: July 24-August 14: Daily 8-6

Montmorency cherries, Morello cherries (limited supply). The Montmorency is a sour cherry grown commercially in North America. The Morello is the dark sour cherry

familiar to Europeans. The farm also has dehydrated
Montmorency cherries for use in baking or snacks.
Fruit is hand-picked, fresh everyday to ensure superior
quality.
Volume discounts are available for purchases of more
than 500 lbs.
Countertop pitters are available to speed the pitting
process and eliminate the drudgery. CHERRY JUBILEE
has published a cookbook featuring more than 32
recipes using the Montmorency cherry.

CHERRYHILL FARM
4133 SELDON ROAD, ABBOTSFORD
PHONE: 859-6352
HOURS: July 1-August 1: Daily 8-6

With about 1,400 trees, this farm offers U-pick, ready-
picked, or picked and pitted. Montmorency cherries
make the most delicious pies, tarts, and jams. They
freeze and preserve beautifully.

CHILLIWACK MILK MAID DAIRY
47582 YALE ROAD EAST, CHILLIWACK
PHONE: 795-3666   FAX: 795-2762
HOURS: 8-5

Offers all sizes of milk, both retail and commercial.
MILK MAID products are produced fresh from their own
dairy herd. 40 flavours of rich gourmet ice cream. As a
small independent dairy they can give personal service

to their delivery customers. Sells retail and will give large volume discounts.

CHILLIWACK PUBLIC MARKET
CORNER VICTORIA/MILL STREET, CHILLIWACK
HOURS: Wed and Sat all year round

An ecclectic group of local food producers and craftspeople.

CHILLIWACK RIVER VALLEY NATURAL HONEY
46171 CHILLIWACK LAKE ROAD, CHILLIWACK
PHONE: 853-3466
HOURS: Daily 9-6

Beekeepers Jack and Agnes Coutts are involved in every step of the honeymaking process, and their efforts continue to produce award-winning products. Their bees create four flavours of honey: Wildflower, Scotch Thistle, Mountain honey, and Fireweed. Bee pollen, honeycomb, candles, and natural propolis tincture are also available at the farm.

CHOCOLATE ARTS
2037 WEST 4TH AVENUE, VANCOUVER
PHONE: 739-0475   FAX: 731-2615
HOURS: Mon-Fri 1:30-6, Sat 10-5:30

Specialty chocolates with distinctive BC fillings. During seasons (ie: Christmas, Easter) the store features a wide array of innovative moulds. Everything is produced on the premises. Original medallion designs by Canadian/Haida artist Robert Davidson are also available (although they are too beautiful to eat.) You can also have custom chocolate sculptures and pieces made for you. Volume discounts are available; prices vary depending on product and amount.

CHOCOLATERIE BERNARD CALLEBAUT
2698 GRANVILLE, VANCOUVER
PHONE: 736-5890

Offering all things sweet and rich, this company is run by a member of the famous chocolate family. The highest quality ingredients result in a variety of tempting delights such as truffles and pralines.

CHOCOLATE MOUSSE KITCHENWARE
1553 ROBSON, VANCOUVER
PHONE: 682-8223
HOURS: Mon-Sat 9-9, Sun 10-7

More than 2,000 square feet of space stocks 15,000 different products, from Icelandic 'Look' cooking pans to fish tweezers. If what you're looking for is hard-to-find this store will probably have it.

CHOCOLATIER
BOX 333 MOUNT MORRIS, IL, 61054

A bi-monthly publication sure to please every chocolate lover.

CHOICES MARKET

2627 WEST 16TH, VANCOUVER
PHONE: 736-0009   FAX: 736-0011
HOURS: Mon-Fri 8-9, Sat 8-7:30, Sun 9-7

Specializes in natural foods, many certified organic
items. Prices are competitive. Monthly newsletter
features information and special products. Coffee, food,
and juice bar. Wide range of organic and medication-
free fish and meat. Join as a member of the CHOICES
club and receive discounts.

CHONG TAI FARM MARKET

9520 STEVESTON HWY, RICHMOND
PHONE: 241-9260
HOURS: Daily 9-6

This farm market is a retail and wholesale outlet for
Chinese and organic vegetables, as well as regular
produce. It has been serving Lower Mainland customers
for 20 years.

CIOFFI'S MEAT MARKET & DELI

4152 HASTINGS, BURNABY
PHONE: 291-9373
HOURS: Mon-Thu 9-5:30, Fri to 9, Sat to 5

Specializes in authentic Italian imported products, as
well as products from Croatia and Germany. The store
also carries beef, veal, baby beef, rabbits, free range
chickens and eggs, quails and turkey. Items are
reasonably priced and in-store specials are available.
Large volume discounts are available on cold cuts and

meats. Family owned and operated by Antonio and Rino Cioffi.

CIRCLING DAWN ORGANIC FOODS
1045 COMMERCIAL, VANCOUVER
PHONE: 255-2326   FAX: 255-2370
HOURS: Daily 10-9

Offers a diverse selection of organically grown produce, grains, beans, pastas and processed foods, organic cheese and oils. Also extensive medicinal, herb, salve and tincture section. Discounts on case lots and whole sack purchases.

CITY FOOD MAGAZINE
RHONDA MAY EDITOR/PUBLISHER
1810 PINE, VANCOUVER
PHONE: 737-7845   FAX: 734-8107

An invaluable resource for food lovers. Chock full of food news, sources, tips and recipes. And it's free.

COMMUNITY SHARED AGRICULTURAL ORGANIZATION
BOX 53577 984 WEST BROADWAY, VANCOUVER

Membership entitles you to organic produce at wholesale prices, delivered to your door.

CONTINENTAL COFFEE
1806 COMMERCIAL DRIVE, VANCOUVER
PHONE: 255-0712

Right on the corner of 2nd Avenue and Commercial, this
family-run business roasts its own beans. A friendly,
low-key place where you can buy whole or ground beans
while sipping a cappuccino. Teas and sweet treats are
also available.

COOKSHOP
CITYSQUARE (12TH AND CAMBIE), VANCOUVER
PHONE: 873-5683

Prep tables and butcher blocks can be found at this
huge (4,000 square foot) store, as well as Bosch kitchen
mixers from Germany and Finnish stainless steel
cookware. At the back of the store, cooking classes are
taught by leading local chefs.

COUNTRY BUMPKINS
41510 NO 3 ROAD, YARROW
PHONE: 823-6844
HOURS: July-November: Fri 3-8, Sat-Sun 8-8

This farm sells fruit, vegetables, nuts and honey. Uses
Integrated Pest Management. Its motto is "Don't Mess
with Mother Nature."

CROFT'S HEALTH PRODUCTS
6262 FRASER STREET, VANCOUVER
PHONE: 324-2121
HOURS: Mon-Sat 10-5:30

Offering both a retail outlet and a mail-order service, Croft's specializes in herbs, vitamins, and minerals, including a full line of made-in-BC products.

CRS WORKERS' CO-OP HORIZON DISTRIBUTION
8335 WINSTON STREET, BURNABY
PHONE: 420-6751   FAX: 420-0178
HOURS: 8:30-4:30

Specializes in packaged, bulk, and frozen natural foods. Superior customer service. Prompt delivery. Knowledgeable staff. The coop handles more than 2,500 items, many of which cater to dietary needs, e.g. wheat-free, gluten-free. Large volume discounts are offered through manufacturer's promotions and trade shows. A worker-owned company.

CSA RESOURCE CENTRE
C/O MAITLAND VALLEY CONSERVATION
BOX 127, WROXETER, ONT N0G 2X0
PHONE: 519-335-3557

Resource for community shared agricultural
organizations.

D

DAVE'S ORCHARD
5910 216TH STREET, LANGLEY
PHONE: 534-9979
HOURS: August-mid March: Daily 9-9

Fruit trees, about 50 different varieties, provide apples,
pears, and peaches. Home-grown fruits and vegetables
are for sale until November; potatoes and apples are

sold through to the spring. Please phone for large
volume orders or to book farm tours.

DAYBREAK FARMS
41212 NO 3 ROAD, YARROW
PHONE: 823-4201   FAX: 823-4449
HOURS: Mon-Fri 8-5 all year round

Free range brown and white eggs. The farm is operated
by John and Darren Bowman.

DELTA FARM MARKET (DELTAPORT)
2757 52ND STREET, LADNER
PHONE: 946-6624
HOURS: Early Feb to New Year's Eve: Daily 8:30-6

Full range of fruits and vegetables with emphasis on
local products as soon as, and for as long as possible.
Fresh produce at low prices, displayed beautifully.
Friendly service. Large volume discounts are available
during canning season.

DIAL- A-DIETITIAN

For answers to questions related to nutrition, call
Kathleen Quinn at 736-2033.

DIVINO'S QUAYSIDE WINE CELLAR
101-810 QUAYSIDE DRIVE, NEW WESTMINSTER
PHONE: 522-4245   FAX: 291-7971
HOURS: 9:30-6:30 seven days a week

Unique and exclusive wines from around the world.
Great selection of dessert and Italian wines.
Great service with knowledgeable staff in a small
European-styled wine shop. Eighty per cent of the
store's wines are exclusive to DIVINO's. Case lot
discounts available on selected products. DIVINO WINE
CELLAR is affiliated with the Divino Estate Winery, New
Westminster's only private wine shop. Manager Stephen
Bonner is a wine writer and educator. The wine cellar
also has an outlet at Robson Public Market.

DOMAINE DE CHABERTON ESTATE WINERY
1064 216TH STREET, LANGLEY
PHONE: 530-1736   FAX: 533-9684
HOURS: Mon-Sat 10-6, Sun 12-5

Nestled in the beautiful countryside of the Fraser Valley,
Domaine de Chaberton found a perfect home for a
vineyard and elegant European style winery. Claude
Violet, who was born in Paris but grew up in the south of
France, brought with him a heritage of grape growing
and fine wine making which dates back to 1644. In July
1991, the Violet family opened their doors to the public
as the Fraser Valley's first commercial vineyard with an
on-site retail store. The newly renovated tasting room,
enlarged to accommodate the increasing crowds of wine
lovers, welcomes you in its warm atmosphere of oak,

stained glass and pewter decor. The friendly and knowledgeable staff will introduce you to a wonderful selection of premium wines.
Hospitality Room - Mon-Sat 10-6
Sun 12-5
Tours (Seasonal) - Sat/Sun 2:00, 3:00, 4:00
Group tours by appointment only.

DRIEDIGER FARMS
23823 72ND AVENUE, LANGLEY
PHONE: 888-1665   FAX :   888-1685
HOURS: June 15-August 15: Daily 8-9

Strawberries, gooseberries, raspberries, blueberries, black and red currants and corn. Quality berries, friendly service. The farm sells by the basket 2.5 lb., 10 lb. and 20 lb. The larger the quantity the lower the price. The Driedigers celebrated their 30th anniversary in the 1994 season. Family-owned and operated.
DRIEDIGER FARMS began its pesticide reduction program in 1979. Since 1985, the farm has been practising Integrated Pest Management.

DRINKWATER AND COMPANY FINE COOKWARE
4465 WEST 10TH AVENUE, VANCOUVER
PHONE: 224-2665
HOURS: Mon-Sat 9:30-5:30

Kitchen gadgets, bakeware, cookware, decorative accessories, Millenium cookware as seen on the Urban

Peasant, handpainted pie plates. The store offers a free
newsletter full of recipes, tips and kitchen hints.

DUBRULLE FRENCH CULINARY SCHOOL
1522 WEST 8TH AVENUE, VANCOUVER
PHONE: 738-3155

Call for a calendar of full and part-time cooking and
baking courses.

DUNLEVY SALES
5 EAST 5TH, VANCOUVER
PHONE: 873-2236   FAX : 873-0899
HOURS: Mon-Fri 8-5:30, Sat 10-3

Restaurant equipment and supplies, commercial ovens,
grills, coolers, freezers, broilers, fryers, toasters, ice
machines, coffee machines, kitchenware, small wares,
cutlery, glassware and chinaware. Quality goods and a
high standard of service. Five per cent discount for
cash and carry. Deals primarily with restaurants, but the
public is welcome to shop here as well.

DUSSA'S HAM AND CHEESE
1689 JOHNSTON STREET ,VANCOUVER
PHONE: 688-8881   FAX: 261-5357
HOURS: 9-6

Cheeses from 28 countries. Ready-to-eat fancy meat
products, mustard and crackers. More than 250
international cheeses. High-quality merchandise and
friendly and knowledgeable staff. Three-year-old

Ontario vintage cheddar, large selection of rare french cheeses, fresh bries and camemberts, goat cheeses, roquefort, tete de moine, swiss and french raclette, comte, cantal, Italian parmesans, gorgonzolla, cambozola, stilton, appenzeller. Volume discounts available for restaurants.

DUTHIE'S BOOKS
919 ROBSON, VANCOUVER
PHONE: 684-4496   FAX: 684-5142
HOURS: Mon-Fri 9-9, Sat 9-6, Sun 12-5

Extensive selection of food books and magazines. Check phone book for other locations.

E

EARTH'S GOOD HARVEST
107-1077 56TH STREET, TSAWWASSEN
PHONE: 943-3035   FAX: 943-3095
HOURS: Mon-Sat 9-6, Sun 12-5

Organic produce, complete selection of alternative grains, fresh ground whole wheat, rye and spelt (grinder in the store). Non-irradiated spices, specialty breads, fresh-baked pies and muffins, gourmet packaged foods.

Personal, knowledgeable, friendly service remembering individual customers and their needs. The store has its own certified organic farm. Organic grains, all produce organic - BC grown when available, alternate flours and grains. A 20 per cent discount available on case lots.

ECCO IL PANE
238 WEST 5TH, VANCOUVER
PHONE: 873-1814 FAX: 873-1835
HOURS: Mon-Fri 8-5, Sat 8:30-5, Sun 9-5

Authentic Italian country breads, biscotti and dolci (sweets, cakes, torta, etc.) The bakery/cafe offers an excellent selection of Italian and country breads made in the traditional style without preservatives, sugar, oil or dairy. Wholesale pricing available for restaurants; retail customers receive discounts on large volume purchases. Even though it is a large scale bakery, everything is done by hand, the way bread used to be made centuries ago. The breads are available in more than four dozen venues within Vancouver and extending to White Rock, Tsawwassen and Victoria.

ECHO'S DISCONTINUED CHINA & SILVER
121-1433 LONSDALE, NORTH VANCOUVER
PHONE: 980-8011

This useful store is your best bet for finding discontinued china or silver patterns. Whether it's a lost fork or a set of salad plates from a hard-to-find dinnerware line, ECHO'S will match buyers and sellers through their registry.

ECOLE DE GASTRONOMIE FRANCAISE
RITZ-ESCOFFIER
15 PLACE VENDOME, PARIS, FRANCE 75001
PHONE: (33) 1-42-60-38-30

Call or write for a current course calendar.

ELIZABETH'S GOURMET DELIGHTS AND CATERING
128 4857 ELLIOTT, LADNER
PHONE: 946-7066
HOURS: Sun-Fri 8-5:30, Sat 9-5:30

ELIZABETH'S cheesecake is second to none. One customer recently wrote to BON APPETIT about it and the recipe was written up in the magazine's RSVP section. ELIZABETH'S also offers homemade soups and a host of wonderous desserts.

ELYSIA HERB FARM
23519 OLD YALE ROAD, LANGLEY
PHONE: 534-5118
HOURS: Mid April-June and w/ends 11-5
         July only by appointment

Spring: Herbal bedding plants. Summer thru early fall: fresh cut herbs if available. Fall through Christmas; dried herbs, herbal products - vinegars, jellies, mustards, seasonings, bath bags. Chemical-free gardening and friendly, informative, personal service.

ERNIE'S AUSTRIAN BAKERY

1210-200TH STREET, LANGLEY
PHONE: 533-5565
HOURS: Tues-Thu 9-7, Fri 9-7:30, Sat 9-6, Sun 10-6

Breads and other baked goods. Rye breads a specialty; caraway rye is the bakery's most sought after. On Saturdays raisin, poppy seed, and sour french bread are featured. This company has been in business for more than 40 years. It started on Kingsway, moved to Alma Street, and finally settled in Langley.

ESPRESSO CAPPUCCCINO COFFEE MACHINE COMPANY

2095 COMMERCIAL, VANCOUVER
PHONE: 254-0711   FAX: 255-4031
HOURS: Mon-Fri 9-6, Sat 9-4

Espresso/cappuccino equipment, as well as other restaurant equipment such as bar counters, pastry displays, pasta machines, ice-cream machines. The store also offers some home machines for espresso/cappuccino, pasta and ice-cream. Quality products, knowledgeable staff, good technical/service support staff. Customer training provided on all machines. All equipment is from Italy. Owners travel frequently to Italy to pick up the latest in restaurant ideas from the Milan Fair.
The company is owned and operated by the Bresciani brothers who came to Canada 30 years ago and "brought a little bit of Italy with them."

EXPRESSOHEAD COFFEE HOUSE
1945 CORNWALL, VANCOUVER
PHONE: 739-1069   FAX: 681-1258
HOURS: Sun to Thur 7-12, Fri, Sat 7-1am

Mochas, Tiger Bombs, Lattes, Cappuccinos,
Americanos, delectable desserts, savoury sandwiches,
home-style soup. It's a great place to meet friends,
play chess, read a book, do homework or just relax on
your own. Features "mile-high lemon meringue pie,"
the "big" chocolate cake, Mario's glory.

EUROPEAN CHEESECAKE FACTORY
UNIT 101-20530 LANGLEY BYPASS, LANGLEY
PHONE: 533-1481   FAX: 538-2481
HOURS: Mon-Sat 10-5:30

The EUROPEAN CHEESECAKE FACTORY makes
high quality desserts. Weekly specials are offered, as
well as discounts on "thrift" (imperfect) cakes, free
samplings on Saturdays, and various seasonal
promotions throughout the year. For large volume
discounts, please phone for details. This company
started as a home-based business 12 years ago and is
now supplying desserts to the food industry across
Canada (plus retail outlets in four locations).

F

FALCONE BROTHERS' MEAT MARKET
1810 COMMERCIAL DRIVE, VANCOUVER
PHONE: 253-6131
HOURS: Mon-Sat 9-5:45

This small store has been a fixture on Commercial Drive
for 27 years. Sausages are the market's specialty,
especially pork (available hot, medium, or mild) and
liver. The brothers also sell fresh rabbits.

FALK'S FARM
187-188TH STREET, SURREY
PHONE: 538-1149
HOURS: August to October

Twenty-five varieties of organically-grown apples.
Regular price is 50 cents a pound. For volumes over
200 pounds, price is negotiable.
Only mechanical pest management is used here. For
example, aphids are dealt with by spraying water with a
high pressure garden hose.

FAMOUS FOODS
1595 KINGSWAY, VANCOUVER
PHONE: 872-3019
HOURS: Mon-Thur & Sat 9-6, Fri 9-9, Sun 10-5

Baking supplies, bulk foods (packaged in small amounts to avoid contamination), spices and herbs, grains and cereals. Dried fruits and vegetables. Friendly willing staff. Competitive prices. Super weekly specials. Wheat-free, gluten-free products. Great variety of herbs and spices.
Large volume discounts available to commercial accounts only. Serving Vancouver for more than 40 years.

FARM FOLK/CITY FOLK
606-1590 WEST 1ST AVENUE, VANCOUVER
ONLINE SERVICE 430-8080 WITH MODEM
PHONE: 731-7785

Non-profit resource network organized to open the communication lines between farmers and consumers. Includes farmers, wholesalers, grocers, chefs, environmentalists, department of agriculture representatives and food writers. Membership also open to anyone with an interest in food or agriculture. This organization hosts farm visits and other food-related events.

FARM FRESH GUIDE

A newsletter published in cooperation with the Township of Langley. Offers information for those who wish to take advantage of the produce and agricultural offerings of the area. Phone 1-604-533-6127.

FAST AND FANTASTIC
DW FRIESEN & SON LTD, 1990
NORTH SHORE FAMILY SERVICES SOCIETY,
NORTH VANCOUVER

Good food recipes for the hurried cook.

FAZIO FOODS INTERNATIONAL LTD
1050 GLEN DRIVE, VANCOUVER
PHONE: 253-2668   FAX: 253-5535
HOURS: Mon-Fri 8-4:30

Canola oil, corn oil, sunflower oil, margarine, shortening, whole tomatoes, crushed tomatoes, tomato paste, chick peas, red kidney beans, olive oil, mayonnaise and much more. Continuous reliable supply. Satisfaction guaranteed. Large volume discounts are available. NOTE: This company does not sell retail.

FINE COOKING
TAUNTON PRESS
63 SOUTH MAIN ST, NEWTOWN CT 06470-5506

Extensive step-by-step instructions, clearly illustrated.
Each volume is a valuable addition to the cook's library.

FINLANDIA PHARMACY
1964 WEST BROADWAY, VANCOUVER
PHONE: 733-5323
HOURS: Mon-Fri 9-6, Sat 10-5, Sun 12-5

Qualified herbal practitioners offer sound advice on
everything from herbal teas and natural energy
boosters, to homeopathic allergy remedies and cruelty-
free cosmetics. Wellness literature is also available from
this large store.

FLAVOURS OF MEXICO
TOUR OF FOOD IN MEXICO
MARILYN TAUSEND
6023 REID DR NW, GIG HARBOUR WASH 98335
PHONE: 206-851-7676

Call for details of upcoming tours.

FORSTER'S FINE CHEESE
2104 WEST 41ST, VANCOUVER
PHONE: 261-5813   FAX : 261-7566
HOURS: Mon-Sat 9:30-5

Hundreds of the world's best cheeses, herbs and spice
blends, pates, lox, condiments, olive oils and balsamics.
Variety, freshness and 30-plus years experience.
Cheeses found nowhere else in Canada: soft cheeses
with bark; very old cheddars from Ontario and England,
many Chevres.
Large volume discounts available.
Supplied cheeses for the royal tour of the Prince and
Princess of Wales in 1986. Exclusively recommended
by Fortnum and Mason, London.

FORSTBAUER FAMILY NATURAL FOOD FARM
49350 PRAIRIE CENTRAL ROAD, CHILLIWACK
PHONE: 794-3999
HOURS: June-February: Mon-Sat 8-8, Sun 1-8

All vegetables at this farm are grown organically.
Produce is available directly from the farm, either pre-
order or U-pick, as well as from the Public Market in
Chilliwack. The Forstbauers offer items such as
Bluelake pole beans, carrots, beets, potatoes, and
pickling cucumbers. Free range eggs, beef, and pork are
also available. Okanagan fruit can also be ordered
through this farm.

FRANK-LYNN BERRY FARMS

23370 50TH AVENUE, LANGLEY
PHONE: 534-2430
HOURS: April-October: Mon-Sat 9-6
PLEASE PHONE in advance

This farm sells berries and fruit that are grown using natural weed and pest control. Ready-picked or U-pick available but please phone to make arrangements. Rhubarb is available April to August; June to October is strawberry season; and raspberries and blueberries are available in June and July.

FRANKE FARMS

48760 YALE ROAD EAST RR#2, CHILLIWACK
PHONE: 792-8601
HOURS: Fri 9-7, Sat 9-5, or call for appointment

Run by Bram and Jenneke Franke.
Potatoes - Yellow Dutch, Pontiac, Yukon Gold, Russets. Sells washed and unwashed potatoes. Large volume discounts available on amounts more than 200 pounds. Uses integrated pest management to minimize chemical use and to produce wholesome and nutritious potatoes.

FRASER VALLEY FARM FRESH PRODUCE GUIDE

Your ticket to the freshest country products sold by local farmers. This guide directs consumers to farm products in the central Fraser Valley, 1-604-823-4311.

FRASER VALLEY SALADMASTER LTD
12-2296 TOWNLINE, CLEARBROOK
PHONE: 857-1460   FAX: SAME
HOURS: Mon-Fri 9-5

Waterless cookware. Cook without water, fats or oils. All
sales done through in-house dinner shows.
Health and nutrition cookware since 1947.
Burnaby Saladmaster - 8026 Enterprise
Central Saladmaster - 302 - 13281 - 78th Ave, Surrey

FROM A COASTAL KITCHEN
LEE REID
HANCOCK HOUSE, 1980

Great fish recipes from a remote fishing village.

FROST HILL FARM
1072 KOSIKAR RD COLUMBIA VAL, LINDELL BEACH
PHONE: 858-7665
HOURS: July-August: full-time
           September-October: Sat-Sun

Run by Bruce and Louise Millar. Fresh from the ground
herbs and garden vegetables, all shapes, all sizes. No
chemicals - just row covers.

FUJIYA FISH AND JAPANESE FOODS
912 CLARK, VANCOUVER
PHONE: 251-3711   FAX: 254-1699
HOURS: Mon-Sat 9-7, Sun 10-7

Japanese foods, books, magazines, kitchenware, lunch boxes, vegetables, fresh tempura. Widest selection of Japanese and Korean food items in Lower Mainland, approximately 20 different Obento (lunch boxes) made daily.
Weekly specials. All kinds of fish including salmon roe and tuna. Pine mushrooms, smoked salmon. Basically anything related to food that is Japanese - this store carries.
Large volume discounts available. Price will vary depending on item and quantity.

Richmond Fujiya - #100 - 8211 Westminster Highway
Tel: 270-3715.
Coquitlam Fujiya - #203 - 403 North Road.
Tel: 931-3713.
Surrey Fujiya - 12849 - 96th Avenue, Townline Plaza
Tel: 581-3732.
Victoria Fujiya - 3624 Shelbourne Street
Tel: 598-3711.
Ocean Delight Seafoods Ltd 450 Alexander Street, Vancouver   Tel: 254-8251.

G

GAIA GARDEN HERBAL APOTHECARY
2672 BROADWAY, VANCOUVER
PHONE: 734-4372
HOURS: Mon-Fri 10-6, Thu 10-8
        Sat 10-5, Sun 12-5

Sells only organically grown herbs. Herbs and herb
extracts are categorized by bottle colour and stored in
oak apothecary cases along the walls. Private
consultations available by appointment. Herb walks and
"wildcrafting" workshops offered as well.

GALLOWAYS SPECIALTY FOODS
1084 ROBSON, VANCOUVER
PHONE: 785-7927
HOURS:

From marzipan to dried beans, to floral gums for cake
decorating or piri piri for the Portugese meal,
GALLOWAYS always seems to have the hard-to-find
products. They carry over 200 herbs and hard-to-find
spices, including sumac and lemon grass (dried,
powdered or fresh), and over a dozen curry powders and
pastes to suit every need. Need a sauce? There are
more than 40 to choose from, originating all over the
world. GALLOWAYS also carries its own line of blended
spices. Other basics such as flour and nuts sold here.

GIRAFFE RESTAURANT
15053 MARINE, WHITE ROCK
PHONE: 538-6878
HOURS: Open 7 days a week after 5pm for dinner.
Lunch: Mon-Fri 11:30
Brunch: Sundays 11am

A daring and everchanging menu, a congenial head chef who takes the time to meet her patrons, and a breathtaking view of the Pacific all combine to make GIRAFFE Tracey's favourite restaraunt. Cooking classes are offered according to seasonal availability of foods.

GLORIOUS GARNISH AND SEASONAL SALAD
PHONE: 857-1400   FAX: 857-1820
HOURS: April-November (phone orders only)

This company sells wholesale only, minimum order of $100. Sells salad combinations, washed and fully prepared. The salads are truly unique in that they are made entirely of edible flowers, wild and cultivated greens, and herbs. Baby vegetables, garnishes, and exotic lettuces also available. Offers large volume discounts through wholesale sales to restaurants and caterers. Certified organic farming. This company occupies three acres of a 10-acre co-operative dedicated to making small farming viable. The members of the company belong to Community Alternatives, a rural-urban co-op. Sells through Valley Organic Farmers at Granville Island.

GOURMET MAGAZINE
560 LEXINGTON AVENUE, NEW YORK NY 10022

Published monthly

GRAEM CASTELL'S FINEST FOODS TO YOUR DOOR
102-1633 WEST 11TH AVENUE, VANCOUVER
PHONE: 731-5456 FAX: 732-3950

Delivery of flash frozen items directly to people's homes anywhere in Greater Vancouver. Graem Castell has a mouth-watering menu of 130 choices including such items as Chicken Cordon Suisse, Stuffed Shrimps, Sole Elite, Buffalo Burgers, delicious Vegetarian Burgers Alberta AAA beef and Deep Dish Triple Chocolate/Peanut Butter. His fish is flash frozen on the boats within two to four hours of being caught. Boxes weigh around two kilograms and contain usually a dozen servings. Everything is totally guaranteed for quality, freezer life and customer's taste. Large volume discounts are available.

GRANVILLE ISLAND MARKET COOKBOOK

A 1995 edition of this favourite will be available soon.

GRANDMAISON BEEF FARM LTD
5175 184TH STREET, SURREY
PHONE: 576-8318   FAX: 576-9340
HOURS: 6-4

Beef, veal and lamb, home-raised packaged on the premises. Selling retail at wholesale prices.

GRANVILLE ISLAND PUBLIC MARKET
GRANVILLE ISLAND, VANCOUVER
PHONE: 666-5784   FAX: 666-7376
HOURS: Daily 9-6
Closed Mondays from Thanksgiving to Victoria Day

Armando's Finest Quality Meats
Bageland
Brussels Chocolates
Buddy's Farm
Candy Kitchen
Coffee Roaster
Daily Grind
Dressed to Go
Duso's Spice Shop
Dussa's Ham and Cheese
Four Seasons Farms
Grainry
Granville Island Produce
Healthy Gourmet
In a Nutshell
Laurelle's Fine Foods
Longliner Seafoods
Milkman
Okanagan Wine Shop
Olde World Fudge

Pacific Rim Shellfish
Pier 8 Deli
Poultryland
Salmon Shop
South China Seas
Stuart's Bakery
Sunlight Farms Tenderland Meats
The Pantry
Turkey Shop
Van Den Bosch Bakery
Zara's Pasta Nest

GRAPE EXPECTATIONS
An annual wine festival. For more information
phone: 270-9463 or 270-7838

GREAT CHEFS AT MONDAVI WINERY
BOX 106, OAKVILLE, CAL 94562
PHONE: 226-1395

A cooking school in California's wine country.

GREAT CULINARY ADVENTURES
(CAREN'S)
1856 PANDORA, VANCOUVER
PHONE: 255-5119   FAX: 253-1331
HOURS: By appointment

Specialty food from caviar to crackers and French
copper cookware. By mail-order or appointment.
Best prices. Truffles, foie gras, caviar, caperberries,
flavored pastas, gold dust, crystalized flowers.

Case lot discounts - 15 per cent.
Vancouver's longest running cooking school. Watch for
Caren's new cookbook.

GREAT WOK CHINESE RESTAURANT
1961 WEST 4th AVENUE
VANCOUVER
PHONE: 739-7668
HOURS: Lunch and dinner Monday through Saturday,
dinner Sunday.

Some of the best Szechuan cuisine this side of The
People's Republic. Specializes in take-out. Good prices,
great food.

GREENDALE APPLE FARM
41905 YALE ROAD WEST, SARDIS
PHONE: 823-4904
HOURS: Open September to February

Apples - Alkamene, Elstar and Jonagold; different
flavours, good for baking and eating.
Fruit is picked, then stored directly in the cooler. It is
handled very little, which limits the bruising. There is no
waxing.
Large boxes purchased (more than 50 lbs) will be
cheaper than smaller quantities.

GREENVALE FARMS
6030 248TH STREET, ALDERGROVE
PHONE: 856-1809
HOURS: June-July: Daily 8-8

For the past 25 years has offered U-pick strawberries.
They also grow raspberries for U-pick and sell picked
blueberries in season.

H

HALAL MEATS & DELI
4413 MAIN STREET, VANCOUVER
PHONE: 879-5518

The word "Halal" refers to the the manner in which an
animal is killed and prepared by a Muslim butcher. No
Muslim would eat any meat that has not undergone the
Halal ritual. HALAL MEATS & DELI offers a large
assortment of meats including: goat, lamb, chicken, and
beef.

HARVEST GUIDE
The guide for fresh produce in "Rainbow Country,"
Chilliwack, BC. Published in association with Agriscope,
1-604-795-8395.

HASTINGS HOUSE
BOX 1110, SALT SPRING
PHONE: 537-2362

For the ultimate getaway HASTINGS HOUSE leaves
nothing to be desired.

HAZELMERE ORGANIC FARMS
1859-184TH STREET, SURREY
PHONE: 538-3018   FAX: 538-3040

HAZELMERE grows and sells most varieties of veggies
that can be grown in the Pacific Northwest. This farm
consistently delivers the highest quality organically
grown vegetables. Pest management involves
disruption of flight patterns of insects, by planting tall
and short plants together and most importantly by
attending to the good health of the soil.
HAZELMERE sells through farm-gate sales as well as
through Capers, Save-on White Rock, Bishop's, William
Tell, Pan Pacific, Four Seasons, Raintree. More than
100 varieties of fruit, vegetables, and herbs.

HEARTS NATURAL FOOD MARKET
3002 GRANVILLE, VANCOUVER
PHONE: 732-4405   FAX: 732-4216
HOURS: Mon-Fri 8-10, Sat 8-8, Sun 9-8

Organic vegetables, high-end deli products, excellent
local bread and bakery products: your all-round high-
quality natural food store.

HEIRLOOM BEAN COMPANY LTD
PO BOX 579, DUNCAN
PHONE: 746-4511
         1-800-4-LENTIL

The HEIRLOOM BEAN COMPANY offers a large
variety of certified organic products through mail order
service. Free delivery is given to orders of over $200.
The aim of this company is to provide a source of
heirloom and other bean varieties from selected farmers
throughout BC and Canada.

HING LOONG
512 MAIN STREET, VANCOUVER
PHONE: 688-3300   FAX: 662-3381
HOURS: 9-6

Housewares, rice cookers and dry foods.
Stock is shipped directly from Hong Kong and China.
Wholesale prices are available.

HING WAH
506 MAIN STREET, VANCOUVER
PHONE: 683-3838   FAX: 662-3381
HOURS: 9-6

Dry foods for cooking, Ginseng and Chinese doctor
prescribed herbal remedies.
Keep fit tea/Korera Ginseng and Ginseng

HODGINS SMITH COUNTRY PRODUCE BARN
39809 N0 3 ROAD, YARROW
PHONE: 852-0888 OR 823-6733
HOURS: May-November: Daily, various hours

Offers a wide selection of fresh fruits and vegetables in season. All vegetables and berries are grown locally. Specializes in growing the sweetest corn. Customers can also purchase fresh farm house bread, homemade fudge, jams, jellies, and fresh fruit pies. Pumpkin tours are arranged in October.

HON'S WUN TUN HOUSE
268 KEEFER STREET
PHONE: 688-0871   FAX: 688-8393
HOURS:

Cantonese food; noodles, wun tun soup with BBQ meats; potstickers, rice, vegetarian dishes, rice dishes, conee, will serve items without msg at request. Fast service, clean open kitchen, almost all food cooked at front counter so customers can see. Retail outlet sells all products made in store: noodles, buns, potstickers, bbq products, dim sum. Started out 22 years ago. Other outlets in Richmond and New West.

HOSTELLERIE DE CRILLON LE BRAVE
SARA MONICK
PLACE DE L'EGLISE 84410 CRILLON DE FRANCE
BRAVE ... Cooking in Provence.
PHONE: 011-33-90-65-61-61

Call or write for calender of upcoming courses.

HOUSE OF BRUSSELS CHOCOLATES
FACTORY OUTLET 208-750 TERMINAL,
VANCOUVER
PHONE: 687-1524   FAX: 687-0142

Creates molded milk, dark, and white chocolates in the
Belgian style, with delectable favourites such as the
hedgehog (filled with chocolate cream), manon
(hazelnut cream in white chocolate), and champagne or
maple truffles.

HOUSE OF KNIVES
476 EAST COLUMBIA,   NEW WESTMINISTER
PHONE: 522-7735   FAX: 522-2748
HOURS: Mall hours

Specializes in all types of high quality kitchen cutlery,
gadgets, scissors and gifts. This company makes a
special effort to search the world every year at the trade
shows to find unique and different items. The staff is
well trained. Has a great selection of brand name
kitchen products and everything they sell is backed with
a lifetime guarantee. Service what they sell. Large
buying power keeps prices reasonable. Special
promotions on most kitchen knives about four times a
year. In-store specials all year round. Unique items
brought recently from Europe include true left-handed
school scissors, a quality bread knife with an adjustable
guard, paring knives with safety covers and fish
tweezers. The HOUSE offers volume discounts on
professional sharpening service for all knives and

scissors. If you bring three or more items at one time you receive 20 per cent off. A VIP discount for all cooking students and professional cooks is offered as well. Family owned and operated business with 10 locations in the province.

Other stores: please phone head office for locations nearest you.

I

IMPERIAL SALMON HOUSE
1632 FRANKLIN, VANCOUVER
PHONE: 251-1114   FAX: 251-3177
HOURS: Mon-Fri 8-4

 Manufactures and sells smoked salmon, both hot and cold (lox), along with other smoked fish products, including Smoked Salmon Butter.
Lox is especially good. Will smoke your sports-caught fish for you.
Smoked salmon butter makes an excellent party gift; salmon jerky is growing in popularity.
Volume discounts are available to businesses only.
A manufacturer/wholesaler but sells over the counter during office hours.

INGREDIENTS ETC
302 20771 LANGLEY BY-PASS, LANGLEY
PHONE: 533-0747
HOURS: Mon-Sat 10-6, Sun 10-5

INGREDIENTS offers a truly international selection of
foods and ingredients including spices, coffees, pastas,
BBQ marinades, and ready made curries. Juniper
berries, saffron, and tzatziki are just a few of the hard-
to-find items that INGREDIENTS sells. Large volume
discounts and unique gift baskets also available.

INTERPORT SALES
418 HADDEN, WEST VANCOUVER
PHONE: 925-3105   FAX: 925-3105
HOURS: Mon-Fri 9-5

Ole Mole gourmet chilies are the specialty of
INTERPORT SALES. A selection of 12 chilies offered in
bulk or beautifully arranged gift baskets. Ole Mole
chilies can be purchased through mail order or a number
of retailers including: Capers, Famous Foods, Hearts,
Herbs and Things, Jody's Catering, Leslie Stowe's,
Pasta Please, and IGA.

ITALCANA IMPORTERS
1288 VERNON DRIVE, VANCOUVER
PHONE: 255-9211   FAX: 253-9798
HOURS: Mon-Fri 9-5, Weekends by appointment

Specializes in espresso coffee machines, coffee
grinders and the Lavazza coffee roaster.

J

JB FOODS
6607 MAIN STREET, VANCOUVER
PHONE: 321-0224
HOURS: Mon-Sat 10:30-6, Sun 11-5

Spices, dals, beans, chutneys, basmati rice and pickles.
Products from India and Pakistan. Gluten-free flours.
Sells a good selection of Indian cookbooks. Large
volume discount prices offered.

JD FARMS SPECIALTY TURKEY STORE
24726 52ND AVENUE, ALDERGROVE
PHONE: 856-2431   FAX: 856-2431
HOURS: Wed-Sat 10-5

Turkeys raised on a natural diet may be ordered for
Thanksgiving, Christmas, and Easter. The farm also has
a new turkey store where a multitude of turkey products
are available. Don't forget to try their famous
homemade turkey sausage.

JACKSON'S MEATS
2214 WEST 4TH AVENUE, VANCOUVER
PHONE: 733-9165
HOURS: Mon-Thu, Sat 9-6, Fri 9-7, Sun 10-6

Owned and operated by the Jackson family since 1911,
this butcher shop offers everything from lamb and veal
to free-range chicken and New York style turkeys. The

deli selection includes cheeses, pates, and the shop's own sausage, most recently the low-fat turkey and veal varieties. Fish is available from the Granville store. Jackson's makes its famous Turkey Royale, which is featured in Western Living magazine every year: the turkey is stuffed with boneless pheasant, boneless chicken, and ground ham, while the neck holds pork sausage and the drumsticks are filled with pork tenderloin. The store offers large volume discounts and will special order any item that you wish.

Granville store: 2717 Granville Street, 738-6328.

JERUSALEM BAKERY / ELMASU MARKET
3477 COMMERCIAL, VANCOUVER
PHONE: 873-2244   FAX: 873-2262
HOURS: 10-7

Specializes in Greek and Mediterranean foods.
Spinach pies and Arabic pastries can be found in the in-store bakery. The store stocks hard-to-find cheeses and olives, deli meats, dried beans and spices, olive oil, falafel mix, bulgur. For 17 years the store has provided excellent service, both retail and wholesale, to the Arabic, Greek, Armenian and Turkish community.

JOSIE'S SPECIALTY FOODS AND DELI
7011 FRASER, VANCOUVER
PHONE: 321-1229
HOURS: Tues-Sun 10-7, Mon 4-7

Whole roasted pig and fresh spring rolls (Lumpiang Sariwa) are some of the Filipino dishes Josie prepares.

Ingredients for Filipino food, desserts and other oriental products are available. Ten years in the business; featured in The Vancouver Sun in June, 1992.

JERSEY FARM
4190 46A STREET, DELTA
PHONE: 946-5311 FAX: 946-5774
HOURS: Mon-Fri 8-5

All jersey milk products, regular and low-fat fruit yoghurts, natural yoghurts in 5%, 2%, and non-fat; devon cream, dairy puddings, tzatziki. The only dairy producing all-jersey products. Jersey milk is higher in non-fat solids such as calcium, phosphorous, and protein than regular milk (Holstein). Occasional specials on items that are close to expiry date. Small containers of yoghurts are sold by case lot only. Products are available through Capers, Choices, IGA, Savon, Safeway, Buy-Low, and other stores in the Lower Mainland.

JURGEN GOTHE/ WORDS AND MUSIC, FOOD AND WINE
400-1445 WEST GEORGIA, VANCOUVER
PHONE: 681-9601

Mr Gothe can be heard and read regularly in a number of Lower Mainland and Vancouver media sources. He has vast oenological knowledge and loves to share this with listeners and readers. "The Cooking Game," the first North American game show based on food and wine, and a series of evenings combining the music of the Vancouver Symphony Orchestra with food and wine stories of various regions of the world are just two of the recent contributions Jurgen Gothe has made to the Vancouver culinary and wine scene.

K

KAM TONG ENTERPRISES LTD
276 EAST PENDER STREET, VANCOUVER
PHONE: 683-0033   FAX: 683-0833
HOURS: Daily 9-6

Retail store provides a huge selection of seafood and meat products to meet the cooking needs of many cultures. Specializes in live seafood (Atlantic lobsters, prawns, crabs, clams, snails, mussels, oysters, scallops, abalone, quillback, geoduck, tilipia, etc) and also carries a good variety of fresh seafood from local and international fishing boats. Frozen seafoods such as pomfret fish from India are available as well. KAM TONG stocks fresh-killed pork, beef and poultry products and exotic items such as alligator and frozen snake meat. All meats are guaranteed for quality and freshness. Will pack seafood and other products for travel. Offers large volume discounts. Second outlet, New Chong Lung Meat Shop, at 595 Gore Avenue, Vancouver, BC V6A 2Z6, ph: 685-3632.

KERRISDALE MEAT MARKET
2070 WEST 41ST, VANCOUVER
PHONE: 261-8755
HOURS: Mon-Sat 9-6

Although this store can provide the cook with a full
range of meat products, from free range turkeys to
English Gammon bacon, its specialty is sausage. Made
on the premises under the supervision of owner/master
sausage-man Robert Goodrick, over 40 types of MSG-
free sausage can be taken home to your table. From a
mild pork and apple sausage to the Hot and Spicy Cajun
Bayou Banger, there is a sausage to meet your needs. A
wide range of meats are used, from turkey and chicken
to pork, beef and lamb. The sausages are 95 per cent
lean meat, with no binders or fillers used. Robert does
sell wholesale, while large volume purchases can be
given a modest discount.

KIN'S FARM MARKET
176-8120 NO 2 ROAD, RICHMOND
PHONE: 275-1401
HOURS: Mon-Thu 9:30-7, Fri 9:30-8, Sat-Sun 9:30-6

From April-October sells BC products and US imports,
from November-March, all products are imported from
around the world. Top quality, friendly service and
reasonable prices. Caselot and restaurant discounts.
First outlet opened in 1987 in Richmond. Stores
selected by The Province and The Richmond Review as
the "Best Place to Shop for Produce."

Other outlets include:

5227-48 Ave, Ladner
Brentwood Mall, Burnaby
Park Royal Shopping Centre South, West Vancouver

KITCHEN SHELF

SEMIAHMOO CENTRE, WHITE ROCK
WILLOWBROOK SHOPPING CENTRE, LANGLEY
(COOKSCHOOL SUPPLIES, PATTI HOWDEN)
PHONE: 531-3522
HOURS: WHITE ROCK - Mon-Wed, Sat 9:30-5:30
                              Thur-Fri 9:30-9:00
                              Sun 12:00-5:00
             LANGLEY   - Mon, Tues, Sat
                              Wed-Fri 9:30-9:00
                              Sun 11:00-5:00

Specializes in kitchen electricals, gadgets, bakeware,
cookware, utensils, decorating equipment, fabrics,
tableware, giftware. All good quality items. Cuisinart,
Kitchenaid, Look Cookware, Denby Tableware, Martin
Beck Tableware, Stymeist Tableware, Portmerion
Tableware.

The KITCHEN SHELF provides consistent,
knowledgeable and friendly service in a helpful
environment. They consistently aim to provide the most
recently available quality, unique gadgets, cookware,
bakeware and tableware. Offers a Bridal/Gift Registry.
Under certain circumstances, gives discounts for large
volume purchases.

The KITCHEN SHELF has been in White Rock for over 20 years with its popular cooking school.

KITSILANO NATURAL FOOD STORE
2582 WEST BROADWAY, VANCOUVER
PHONE: 734-1822

Offer the finest of health foods available. No preservatives. Specializes in organic produce, vegetables, flours, grains and food stuffs. Ten per cent discount offered to seniors every day. Delivery service throughout Vancouver. Sells vitamins, herbs, cosmetics, toiletries, books and sandals. Owner operated.

KOHLER'S EUROPEAN SAUSAGE LTD
3338 272ND STREET, ALDERGROVE
PHONE: 856-4151
HOURS: Mon-Fri 7:30-5:30

Manufactures a full line of European speciality meats along with a good selection of fresh meats. Factory-direct prices, quality and freshness. Prices are reasonable and large volume discounts are available depending on the product and quantity. This family-owned business has been producing sausage and ham products for more than 50 years. The company started in Berlin, Germany, which is why they have the Berlin Bear in their logo.

KRAUS BROS FARMS
6179 248TH STREET, LANGLEY
PHONE: 856-5757 FAX: 856-5725
HOURS: June-Sept: Mon-Sat 8-8, Sun 9-6

Strawberries are available in mid-June; then U-pick or
ready-picked raspberries; picked blackberries,
blueberries, everbearing strawberries, cucumbers, corn,
and other vegetables.
The strawberries are all everbearing varieties, and are
grown on raised beds which results in a clean fruit.

L

LA BAGUETTE ET L'ECHALOTTE
1680 JOHNSTON, VANCOUVER
PHONE: 684-1351   FAX: 684-1352
HOURS: Tues-Sun 8am-6pm

LA BAGUETTE is a French bakery and pastry shop,
specializing in French bread and French pastries,
chocolate, and wedding cakes. Special attention to
details, products and a big attention to customers with
the service. LA BAGUETTE is a pioneer in doing
breads with no yeast, no fat, no sugar, no preservatives,
no additives. The company supplies a number of hotels
and restaurants at wholesale prices. In business since
1982.

LA BELLE AUBERGE RESTAURANT
4856 48TH AVENUE, LADNER
PHONE: 946-7717   FAX: 276-2651
HOURS: Tues-Sat 6-12pm,
      Brunch: Sun 11-2
      Dinner Buffet: 5-12

This is French Cuisine at its best. Fifteen years in the same location with consistently excellent food. Three, five and seven course "Gastronomic Dinners" of European quality are available. Bruno Marti, owner and chef, was on a Culinary team of five chefs that won a World Championship at the Culinary Olympics held every four years in Frankfurt, Germany.

LA CASA GELATO
1033 VENABLES, VANCOUVER
PHONE: 251-3211   FAX: 251-3922
HOURS: 12-10

LA CASE GELATO is the producer of premium ice creams, sherbets, sorbettos, and yoghurts for hotels, restaurants and caterers. This company uses the unique Italian "no air" process, which produces an ice cream of silky texture and unmatched flavour; as well this process allows the ice cream to remain frozen and creamy longer than other brands. Made in small batches from special recipes, LA CASA products use only natural ingredients: whole milk, fresh fruits, and pure chocolate. The gourmet flavours of LA CASA GELATO, cover the spectrum of exotic tastes and essences, from luscious Fijian Mango to decadent Chocolate Super Montego Bay.

LA GROTTA DEL FORMAGGIO
1791 COMMERCIAL, VANCOUVER
PHONE: 255-3911
HOURS: Mon-Thu, Sat 9-6, Fri 9-8, Sun 9:30-5

Specializes in cheeses from around the world, pastas, homemade sausages, olive oil. Truly unique selection of both Italian and continental foodstuffs. European store atmosphere and friendly service. Hard- to-find items include truffle pasta, black squid ink pasta, merquez (lamb sausage), goat cheese, truffle olive oil, first cold pressed olive oil. Offers large volume discounts to restaurants and catering orders. The owner brought his skills from Italy via Montreal. The shop has been open for more than 17 years.

LA TOQUE BLANCHE & GOURMET CATERING
4368 MARINE DRIVE, WEST VANCOUVER
PHONE: 926-1006   FAX: 926-1063
HOURS: 5:30 pm onwards

Specializes in GOOD FOOD. Food is consistently well prepared and tasty, with a cozy atmosphere and friendly service. On the catering side, the canapes and open-faced sandwiches are very eye-appealing as well as delicious. Desserts beautifully presented. Ten years ago, Gourmet Catering Services started out in a small kitchen on the North Shore. One of the company's first assignments was catering to a Japanese film crew and cooking for Sean Connery. By Christmas '94 they hope to have their line of vinaigrettes on the shelves of specialty shops.

LA VARENNE SUMMER SCHOOL CHATEAU DU FEY

VILLECCIEN, 89300, JOIGNY, FRANCE
17TH CENTURY CHATEAU...WINE COUNTRY
PHONE: (33) 86-63-18-34

Call or write for details of upcoming courses.

LAZY GOURMET

1595 WEST 6TH AVENUE, VANCOUVER
PHONE: 734-2507   FAX: 734-5877

One of Vancouver's first take out gourmet stores. The sticky buns and nanaimo bars are famous throughout the Lower Mainland. Catering available upon request.

LE CHOCOLATE BELGE DANIEL

124 WEST 3RD, VANCOUVER
PHONE: 879-7782

Secret recipes from Belgium have contributed to the success of this chocolate store, which has won local awards and honours for its products. Uses natural ingredients only.

LE CORDON BLEU

8 ET 8 BIS LEON DELHOMME, FRANCE
75015 PARIS
PHONE: (33) 1-48-56-06-06

Call or write for more information and course calenders.

LE CORDON BLEU PARIS COOK SCHOOL
400 1390 PRINCE OF WALES DRIVE, OTTAWA, ONT
K2C 3N6
PHONE: 224-8603   FAX: 224-9966

Contact the school for course information.

LE MANOIR AUX QUATRE-SAISONS
GREAT MILTON, OXFORD, OX44 7PD
ENGLAND
LE PETIT BLANC ECOLE DE CUISINE
PHONE: 011-44-844-278881
FAX: 011-44-844-278847

Contact the school for course details and schedules.

LE MERIDIEN CHOCOLATE BAR
845 BURRARD, VANCOUVER
PHONE: 682-5511
HOURS: Thu 6-10, Fri-Sat 6-11

Mmmmm! A must for chocolate lovers.

LEE'S CANDIES
4361 WEST 10TH, VANCOUVER
PHONE: 224-5450
HOURS: Mon-Sat 10-5

Specializes in homemade chocolates with special
moulds used for every holiday. Also known for friendly
and courteous service, offering a mouthwatering piece

of chocolate free with every purchase. Unique also to the Lower Mainland is a delicious peanut butter square. LEE'S is hard to find, but just look for the tiny black and white awning and the smiling customers leaving with their treasure bags.

LESLEY STOWE FINE FOODS
1780 WEST THIRD (AT BURRARD), VANCOUVER
PHONE: 731-3663   FAX: 731-3666
HOURS: Mon-Fri 9:30-6:30, Sat 9:30-6, Sun 10-5

Specialty foods; prepared entrees, salads, vegetables, soups, breads, desserts, imported products (ie: olive oils, mustards, pasta, coffee), and Gift Baskets. Unique, high quality, hard-to-find products. Catering for parties from 10 to 500 guests. Known for desserts - original creators of "Death By Chocolate" and Amazing Wedding Cakes. Candied pansies, Nielsen & Massey vanillas, Dean & Deluca spices, chocolate covered cherries and blueberries, dried wild mushrooms, more than 20 varieties of olive oils and one of the best selections of aged balsamic vinegars in the city. The company has catered parties as far away as Newfoundland and shipped its products from Los Angeles to Ireland.

LIBERTY WINE MERCHANT
560-333 BROOKSBANK (PARK&TILFORD)
NORTH VANCOUVER
PHONE: 738-7801   FAX: 739-7800
HOURS: Mall hours

Wine, ciders, coolers, wine accessories, port, sherry and rare old vintages. Liberty offers expert advice and consultations. Excellent selection of California wines, Burgundies, and Bordeaux. Specializes in rare, unusual, great wine at affordable prices. A variety of discounts available on their special wines. Books, accessories, and Reidel wine glasses also sold. Established 1986. Extended hours.

Park Royal South, West Vancouver
Lonsdale Quay, North Vancouver
Park and Tilford, North Vancouver
Hillside Mall, Victoria

LIGHTHEARTED COOKING
ANNE LINDSAY
MACMILLAN, TORONTO, 1994

Heart smart cooking.

LONDSDALE QUAY MARKET
123 CARRIE CATES COURT, NORTH VANCOUVER
PHONE: 985-6261
HOURS: Daily 9:30-6:30, Fri til 9

Bob the Butcher
Bumpkins Country Chicken
Chateau Bakery and Conditorei
Cheesesteaks Plus
Daily Scoop Ice Cream Parlour
Duso's
Garibaldi's Espresso
KRW Turkey Shop
Ken's Produce
La Tortilleria
Liberty Wine Merchants

Lindini's Pizza and Pasta
Mariko Japanese Food and Sushi
Market Fish and Chips
Market Place Deli
Miriam's Ice Cream and Scones
Muffin Delight
New England Pie Company
Odysea Foods
Olde World Fudge Company
Pastel's Restaurant
The Roll Kitchen
Salmon Shop
Sweet Carrie's Dessert Shop
Tino's Bakery

LOONG FOONG BAKERY
247 KEEFER, VANCOUVER
PHONE: 688-0837

This bakery offers counter service and also has a small
back room where you can eat your baked goods with a
cup of tea. Their specialty is sweet cocktail buns and
red, black, or lotus bean cakes. Pork buns and egg tarts
are also sold. Birthday and wedding cakes made to
order.

LOWLAND HERB FARM
5685 LICKMAN ROAD, SARDIS
PHONE: 858-4216
HOURS: Fri-Sat 8-8 ...or call

Boni Townsend has decades of experience in growing
herbs for the wholesale, retail, and nursery markets.
This U-pick garden has been organic for 23 years, while

practising Biodynamics for the past 19. The season lasts
from May to October. Free herb classes and herb teas
by arrangement.

LOX ROYALE
2114 COMMISSIONER STREET, VANCOUVER
PHONE: 251-9844
HOURS: Mon-Fri 8-5

Supplies sockeye, spring, smoked salmon or smoked
Alaska black cod to places like Capers, Pan Pacific, and
Bishops. Offers wholesale as well as retail from their
dockside office on the waters of Burrard Inlet. A
complete line of kosher fish products, as well as
kippered salmon and smoked Indian candy.

M

MAKARA FARMS
5331 RIVERSIDE ROAD, MATSQUI
PHONE: 859-4797   FAX: 859-0531
HOURS: July10- August 20 daily

This family-owned and operated farm sells ready-picked
blueberries guaranteed for freshness, or your money is
refunded. The large, third-generation operation prides
itself on service and quality, and uses biological controls
combined with timely applications of pesticides.
Discounted prices are offered for bringing own
containers. Purchases of 100 lb. or more receive a five
per cent discount, and commercial discounts are
available by individual quote.

MARCELLA & VICTOR HAZAN'S MASTER CLASSES IN ITALIAN COOKING
BOX 285, CIRCLEVILLE NY   10919
16TH CENTURY PALAZZO IN VENICE, ITALY

Write for a calendar of cooking courses.

MARINER MEATS LTD
5229B LADNER TRUNK ROAD, LADNER
PHONE: 946-7511   FAX: 946-7570
HOURS: 10-6

This store specializes in properly aged and trimmed
Grade A beef, fresh pork, lamb and poultry, full deli
meats, cheeses and its own gourmet meat pies and
hamburger patties. Friendly customer service. Custom-
ordered meat, poultry and deli items available.
Wholesale prices available on all products.

MARIO'S GELATI
235 EAST 5TH, VANCOUVER
PHONE: 879-9411   FAX: 879-0435

Now available only by wholesale, MARIO'S GELATI still
makes special flavours such as rose blossom sorbet and
green tea ice cream. The Pan Pacific, among others,
orders frozen desserts from this producer, which also
sells frozen yoghurts.

MARK ANTHONY WINE MART
15220 NORTH BLUFF ROAD, WHITE ROCK
PHONE: 538-9463

 Memo sheet published detailing new or unusual wines,
most priced around $20. Wine accessories.

MARKET AT PARK ROYAL
MARINE DRIVE AND TAYLOR WAY, WEST
VANCOUVER
HOURS: Mon-Wed, Sat 9:30-6, Thur-Fri 9:30-9
          Sun 10-6

Black Forest Delicatessen
Cappuccino Kitchen
Cinful Nature
Fraserview Produce
Herbs and Things
House of Brussels Chocolates
Kin's Farm Market
Liberty Wine Merchants
Naturally Good Foods
Pasta Works
Peter Black and Sons
Van den Bosch Bakery
Waggott's Seafood

MARKET KITCHEN
#2-1666 JOHNSTON STREET, GRANVILLE ISLAND
PHONE: 681-7399
HOURS: Daily 9-6

Specializes in cookware, bakeware,
espresso/cappuccino machines and french porcelain.

The knowledgeable staff (who also love to talk about food) try to emphasize the wonderful fresh products that are available from Granville Market. Extensive bakeware selection, heavyweight French copper. The store also carries Cuisinart food processor spare parts. The MARKET KITCHEN's cooking school ran for five years allowing them to test and demonstrate all of their products.

MARQUIS WINE CELLAR
1034 DAVIE STREET, VANCOUVER
PHONE: 684-0445   FAX: 684-2471
HOURS: Mon-Wed 12-8, Thu-Sun 12-9

Wines, ciders, ports, sherries and champagne, and other wine related merchandise. They also feature Riedel Glassware. Specialize in hard -to-find wines from small, high quality producers. Buyer travels extensively each year, tasting all the wines from cask, before purchasing them for the shop. Extensive knowledge of wine regions and areas. Free delivery of wine - one case minimum to most parts of Vancouver. Chilled wine available. VISA/MC and debit card accepted. Winemaker dinners held at some of Vancouver's finest restaurants. Newsletter and catalogue are also available upon request.

MARVELLOUS MUSHROOMS
20259 50TH AVENUE, LANGLEY
PHONE: 856-3339   FAX: 856-3339

Pesticide free. A perfect place to find oyster and shiitake mushrooms, as well as Asian pears (Pear Apples). The

farm also sells mushrooming kits for enthusiastic
growers to start their own home crop.

MAX'S DELI & BAKERY
3105 OAK STREET, VANCOUVER
PHONE: 733-4838   FAX: 875-8557
HOURS: Daily 6:30-midday

Homemade sauces, healthy nutritious west coast
cuisine, Fichi (fig and anise) bread, two olive bread, Tre
Fromeggi (three cheeses) bread. Incredible selection,
more than 250 items in the deli case. Friendly and
outgoing staff work hard to maintain the reputation that
has earned MAX'S 'Best Deli' three years in a row. A
wide range of Kosher products and speciality breads are
available. No preservatives or additives are used.
Since 1949, MAX'S has enticed, tempted and spoiled
Vancouverites with delectable deli dishes, authentic
knishes, fabulous potato latkes, and ecclectic
assortment of healthy salads and dips, and more than
40 varieties of fresh baked breads.

MAXIM'S BAKERY & RESTAURANT
257 KEEFER STREET, VANCOUVER
PHONE: 688-6281   FAX: 688-CAKE (2253)
HOURS: Daily 8-7

Hong Kong style buns, fresh whipped cream cake. Daily
fresh products, beautifully-designed cakes including
special designs and extra large (300 people) cakes.
Wedding cake rental service and delivery available.

Ask about large volume discounts. MAXIM'S has been
in business for 15 years.

THE MELODIOUS ORCHARD (WALTEN FARM)
51693 OLD YALE ROAD, ROSEDALE
PHONE: 794-3841   FAX: 794-3520
SEASON: September-February/March
HOURS: Mon-Sat 8-8 (phone ahead)

This small organic farm offers Elstar, Jonagold, and
Boskoop apples as well as apple juice and homemade
apple pie. It uses a unique sound and fertilizer program
to enhance crop quality and growth. U-pick or ready
picked. Large volume discounts can be negotiated. The
owners are planning to expand their farm with more
apple varieties (Liberty, Gala, and Cox Orange Pippin)
and free-range eggs and chicken. Retail outlets include
Capers, Pro Organics, and Wild West stores.

MING WO
23 EAST PENDER, VANCOUVER
PHONE: 683-7268   FAX: 683-3848
HOURS: Mon-Sat 9-6, Sun 11-5

High end professional cookware: Calphalon, All Clad,
Cuisinart, Le Creuset, and Lagostina. Offers a wide
selection of basic kitchen utensils and hard-to-find
gadgets, extensive range of bakeware and cake
decorating supplies, specializes in oriental products --
woks, cleavers, clay pots, sukiyaki pans. Also a wide
range of quality knives -- Henckels, Victorinox and
Sabatier. The friendly, knowledgeable staff, try to supply
customers with the right products for their specific needs

and lifestyles. Competitive pricing and seasonally featured sales. Free Henckel knife sharpening clinics twice a year, mail order service for out of town customers. Professional and commercial discounts at the Chinatown location, please phone for details. MING WO is Vancouver's original cookware store. A family-run business since 1917.

Other stores:

4th Avenue 2170 West 4th, Vancouver
737-2624
Capilano Mall 35-935 Marine Drive, North Vancouver
980-9213
Granville 2707 Granville, Vancouver
737-7885
Lansdowne Park 642-5300 No.3 Road, Richmond
270-3732
Lougheed Mall 120-9855 Austin Ave, Burnaby
421-0842
Metrotown   131-4800 Kingsway, Burnaby
435-4640
Motiv   2064 West 4th Ave,   Vancouver
737-8116
Surrey   320-3370 Surrey Place Mall, Surrey
585-2331
Victoria   547 Johnson Street, Victoria
480-0028

MOOSEWOOD COOKBOOK
MOLLY KATZEN
10 SPEED PRESS, CALIFORNIA

The first in a series of vegetarian cookbooks written by
Molly Katzen. The recipes are imaginative enough to
satisfy even devoted meat eaters.

MUM'S ITALIAN GELATO
855 DENMAN STREET, VANCOUVER
PHONE: 681-1500

In business in the West End for more than 10 years,
MUM'S ice cream is popular in both summer and winter.
MUM'S offers traditional flavours as well as special
blends such as baci (chocolate and hazelnut) and
malaga (Spanish wine and raisins).

MURCHIES TEA & COFFEE
1200 HOMER STREET, VANCOUVER
PHONE: 662-3776   FAX: 662-8285
HOURS: 8-5

Speciality coffees, rare teas, spices and hot chocolate.
Quality products and knowledgeable service. Coat of
arms in honour of quality in product and service. 100
years of expertise in blending teas and coffees.
Canada's largest and oldest tea specialists.
Other outlets include:
970 Robson
1030 West Georgia
850 North Park Royal, West Vancouver
City Square, 12th and Cambie
Windsor Square, White Rock

Richmond Centre
5000 Kingsway

MY THAI RESTURANT
118-4061 200TH STREET, LANGLEY
PHONE: 534-2200
HOURS: Lunch: Tues-Sat 11:30-2:30, Sun 12-3
Dinner: Mon-Sat 5-9

Authentic Thai food prepared with the freshest
ingredients. The head chef of MY THAI originally
worked as cook to the Royal Family of Thailand.

N

NATIONAL CHEESE COMPANY
7278 CURRAGH, BURNABY
PHONE: 437-8561   FAX: 437-0117
HOURS: 8:30-4:30

Domestic and imported cheeses from around the world.
Parent company manufactures: Tre Stelle and Cremona
Brand, provolone, havarti, mozzarella, mascarpone,
cream cheese, ricotta, feta, bocconcini, brick, butter,
monteray jack, cheddar. Imports brie, camembert,
swiss, asiago, parmesan, romano, gruyere. Carries one
of the largest variety of cheese products as well as other
food products including: Italian pastas, cured meat
products, imported mineral water and sodas, biscuits,
oils, olives. Excellent service, trucks delivering daily.
Will pre-order specialty perishable cheeses. Prices can
be negotiated for large case lot purchases or will sell by
case or piece. Products may be purchased in all major

chain stores and there is a retail outlet in the warehouse. Tre Stelle products have consistently won gold, silver and bronze medals in various dairy competitions.

NAZARE BBQ CHICKEN
1859 COMMERCIAL DRIVE, VANCOUVER
PHONE: 251-1844
HOURS: Daily 12-7

Excellent take-out or eat-in free-range chicken, roasted slowly on a rotisserie and marinated with spicy or not-so-spicy garlic/vinegar sauces. Served with beans and rice. Very reasonable prices for whole, half, or quarter chickens.

NINE MILE GARDENS
NINE MILES FROM SPENCES BRIDGE ON HWY #8
PHONE: 458-2284
HOURS: Mid July-October daily 8-7

Tomatoes, sweet and hot peppers, eggplant, melons, early potatoes and most garden vegetables. Sells directly to the consumer and gives personal service. Practices organic farming. They have a pound or kilo price as well as a box price for most produce. Ready-pick and U-pick tomatoes and some peppers. Have been growing and selling vegetables in this location since 1977.

NORALL ENTERPRISES
32744 KING ROAD, ABBOTSFORD
PHONE: 852-1790
HOURS: 8-5...Please call

Sells kiwi-grapes, a small grape-sized kiwi fruit with a hairless skin and a sweet, tangier taste than the regular kiwi fruit. They are eaten just like a grape, and used for desserts, salads, and snacks. Kids love them.
Available ready-picked or call ahead for U-pick.

NORTHWEST PALATE MAGAZINE
BOX 10860, PORTLAND, OREG 97210
PHONE: 224-6039   FAX: 222-5312

Bi-monthly publication exploring the Pacific Northwest. Recipes, reviews and food news.

NOT JUST DESSERTS
1638 EAST BROADWAY, VANCOUVER
PHONE: 877-1313

In addition to soups and savoury meals the business is known for its "mile-high" lemon meringue pie, frangelico mousse cake, and Sin City, a chocolate ganache cake served in portions good enough for two.

O

OKANAGAN WINE FESTIVAL
PHONE: 492-6119

Call for details about the 1995 festival.

OLIVIERI FOODS
1906 COMMERCIAL, VANCOUVER
PHONE: 255-8844

In business for more than 30 years, OLIVIERI'S has
been serving fresh pasta and sauces to Vancouver's
food lovers through both retail and wholesale. Also sold
are deli meats, olive oils, and Italian herbs. Original
recipes are still used for their products, and new items
such as lemon-pepper linguine and heat-and-serve
dishes are now available.

ONLY ORIANA
101-1530 WEST 8TH AVENUE, VANCOUVER
PHONE: 731-1391   FAX: 731-0115

This company specializes in healthy gourmet foods and
is directed primarily to the wholesale market. However,
certain items can be bought at the shop, though it is best
to phone ahead. Carries a variety of herbed olive oils,
Asian oils, dressings and marinades. Condiment
delicacies such as Feta Truccata and three-flavoured
pesto are also made. ONLY ORIANA caters to delis,
coffee shops, art galleries, and private and corporate
functions. Currently their products are sold at The Bay,
Big News, O-Tooz, and Charlie's Wine Cellar (Burnaby).

143

P

P AND G SAUSAGE
108-20551 LANGLEY BYPASS, LANGLEY
PHONE: 533-1990
HOURS: Mon-Fri 7:30-5:30, Sat 7:30-5

Known for not using fillers, binders and meat by-products. Everything is made in-house. Large volume discounts offered at owner's discretion. Many varieties of sausage including smoked turkey breast.

PACE'S GOURMET MEATS
16-2565 BARNET HWY, COQUITLAM
PHONE: 942-9996   FAX: 469-7018
HOURS: Mon-Sat 9-6

This store sells only the best Canada Grade "A" fully-aged trimmed to perfection roasts and steaks. Chicken breasts are de-boned, skinned and halved, and trimmed of all visible fat.
This is a cozy, old-fashioned butcher shop complete with wooden floors. Presentation of product and "to the car" service are everyday aspects of the shop. Homemade sausages and Cordon Bleu are routinely made using no fillers, binders, or MSG. Buffalo, venison, ostrich, and other unique items are available upon request.
This store also offers South African products such as Biltong, and in the deli they feature home-cooked roast beef and a wonderful honey-glazed boneless pork loin roast. Large volume discounts on pork chops and beef

stew orders of 5lb or more ($1/lb off) and hamburger and chicken breast large volume orders are subject to various discounts.
Remember: Wednesdays 10 per cent off everything.

PACIFIC NORTHWEST: THE BEAUTIFUL COOKBOOK
KATHY CASEY: EDITOR
WELDON OWEN INC, 1994, SAN FRANCISCO

A culinary journey complete with beautiful photographs.

PAN'S GARDEN
2630 WESTHAM ISLAND ROAD, DELTA
PHONE: 946-0583   FAX: 943-3035
HOURS: Seasonal by appointment

In Greek mythology Pan is the god of nature. This store specializes in herbs and salad crops--produce and specialty items all certified organic. Quality, fresh from farm to store. Large volume discounts available for basil and garlic (reserve early). No agrichemicals used in 14 years.

PAPI'S RISTORANTE ITALIANO
12251 NO.1 ROAD (STEVESTON), RICHMOND
PHONE: 275-8355
HOURS: Lunch: Tues-Sun 11:30-2
       Dinner: Daily 5:30-9:30

This is Italian cuisine at its finest. All pastas are made on the premises and have that melt-in-your-mouth quality. Seafood creations are a speciality.

PARAGON FOOD EQUIPMENT
760 EAST HASTINGS, VANCOUVER
PHONE: 255-9991   FAX: 251-3372
HOURS: Mon-Fri 8:30-5

Specializes in glassware, chinaware, flatware,
pots/pans, knives, kitchen utensils, plasticware, ranges,
coolers, dishwashers, freezers, mixers.
The store carries a large inventory of durable
commercial-quality kitchen equipment. Knowledgeable
staff and large showroom. Monthly specials.
Commercial quality for home use. Case lot discounts,
cash and carry discount. Some items such as china,
flatware, and glasses by the dozens only. Canadian
owned family business. Other outlets: Polygon Metal
Works, 290 West 3rd Avenue, and The Used Food
Equipment Centre, 34 East 2nd Avenue, Vancouver.

PARTHENON SUPERMARKET
2968 WEST BROADWAY, VANCOUVER
PHONE: 733-4191   FAX: 734-4171
HOURS: Mon-Sat 9:30-7:30
          Sun&Holidays 10-6

Importers and distributors of Mediterranean specialty
items like olive oil, olives, feta cheese, tahini, halva,
greek gruyere cheese and hard and soft ricotta, pressed
greek yoghurt, oregano, sage, stuffed vine leaves, fruit
jams, coffee.
A wide variety of low-priced, quality items, combined
with excellent service and Greek music that makes you
want to dance in the aisles.

146

The company imports directly so it can offer goods at discounted prices. PARTHENON supplies many restaurants, supermarkets and distributors in BC. Large volume discounts offered on case lots and even better deals if you buy more cases at a time. PARTHENON has been in business for almost 30 years and is very well known to the community. The store conducts it's wholesale operation from a 5,000 square foot warehouse in Richmond.

PATELS
2210 COMMERCIAL DRIVE, VANCOUVER
PHONE: 255-6729   FAX: 255-8151
HOURS   Mon-Thur 9:30-7
            Fri-Sat 9:30-7:30
            Sun& Holidays 12-6

Specializes in bulk and health foods. Established in 1973 PATELS serves the communities of: Afro-Carribean countries, Central America, China, India, Italy, Indonesia, Latin America, Middle East, Far East, Phillipines, Sri Lanka, Spain, Thailand. PATELS offers extraordinary diversity, marketing fresh tropical delectables, East Indian essentials, tropical produce, goat meat, rice, beans, lentils, spices, pickles, oils, curries, condiments, nuts and raisins, honey, mustard, soups, more than 30 varieties of herbal teas, vitamins, soft drinks from all over the world, cook books.

PATISSERIE BORDEAUX
3675 WEST 10TH, VANCOUVER
PHONE: 731-6551
HOURS Tues-Fri 7-7, Sat-Sun 7-6

All baking done on the premises, recipes are made from
scratch, with the best ingredients and products
available. Excellent quality, service and presentation.
Makes croissants, baguettes, french pastries, cakes,
mousse cakes, fruit flans, and petit fours. For Christmas
they made Bucher de Noel, Croquembouche and
tortieres. Cakes for special occasions made to order.

PATISSERIE BRUXELLES INC. (D.C.DUBY)
1463 HUNTER STREET, NORTH VANCOUVER
PHONE: 980-6776   FAX: 980-6790
HOURS: Mon-Fri 9-4 (pick up between 10:30 & 4)

Specializes in innovative European pastries (Nouvelle
Patisserie); organic ingredients; culinary and medicinal
mushrooms. Wholesome all natural pastry including the
latest European trends. Also provides advice on dessert
wines and will suggest complimentary vintages with your
dessert purchase. Sells at wholesale prices, extra
discount is offered on volume purchases. Some
products available from stock; otherwise the rest of the
product line is available with 48 hours notice. Rush
orders can be arranged for a five per cent surcharge.
The baking chef trained under "Gaston Lenotre" in Paris
and worked at Patisserie Wittamer in Bruxelles; former
member of Vancouver's Culinary team; winners of
national and international medals including gold medal
at Culinary World Cup 1990.

Organically grown mushrooms will be offered in late '94. Varieties include Lion's Mane, Maitake, Shiitake, King Eryngi, and Ling Chi-Reishi.

PERESTROIKA PRODUCE
8626A JOFFRE AVENUE, BURNABY
PHONE: 451-0606   FAX: 451-1849
HOURS: Mon-Fri 6-4

Fully cooked piroshki, with beef potato and onion, cheese, broccoli. Russian heavy 1kg breads (whole wheat, white, rye). Borsch all-vegetable soup. Mini one-inch perogies and beef pelmeni. All products are made on the premises and only the freshest and best ingredients are used in the manufacturing of these delightful products. Volume discount: 10 per cent off on orders over $100. This company is a family-owned business. Other outlet: Babushka's Kitchen in the Granville Island food court.

PIKE PLACE MARKET
1ST AVENUE & PIKE, SEATTLE, WASH
HOURS: Mon-Sat 9-6, Sun 11-6

A fun food experience loaded with surprises. Worth a trip to Seattle.

PINK PEPPERCORN BOOKSTORE
2686 WEST BROADWAY, VANCOUVER
PHONE: 736-4213
HOURS: Mon-Sat 10-5:30, Sun 12-4

Cookbooks for food lovers and the professional.
Vancouver's only complete cookbook store. Cooking
videos for rent. Health, diet, diabetic, and vegetarian
cookbooks. Carries local and international cooking and
baking books. Offers a quarterly newsletter and mail
order services.

POLONIA SAUSAGE
2434 EAST HASTINGS, VANCOUVER
PHONE: 251-2239

Specializes in old fashioned European made sausage.
Quality and taste of pure sausage: no filler.

PRO ORGANICS
3454 LOUGHEED HIGHWAY, VANCOUVER
PHONE: 253-6549

This company supplies organic produce to many of the
Lower Mainland's natural food stores. PRO ORGANICS
is open to the public on Saturdays only.

PUDDIFOOTS
2350 WEST 41ST AVENUE, VANCOUVER
PHONE: 261-8141

Specializes in tableware and kitchen accessories. Two
floors offer everything from top-of-the-line products,
such as Thomas and Rosenthal, to bargain deals on
sturdy china and glassware in the basement. Take your
time to explore this shop, which has been a part of
Kerrisdale's retail strip for years.

PURDYS
2777 KINGSWAY(head office) VANCOUVER
PHONE: 430-4523   FAX: 430-9226
HOURS: Head office: Mon-Fri 9-5

Specializes in assorted chocolates, confections, freshly
roasted nuts and ice cream. Large volume discounts:
10 per cent off orders of $275, 15 per cent on $450, 20
per cent on $700. At Christmas, Group Purchase Plan
offers customers the chance to pool their buying power
and receive 25 per cent of Christmas products. Retail
sales through PURDYS' chocolate retail stores.

Q

QUE PASA
3315 CAMBIE, VANCOUVER
PHONE: 874-0064
HOURS: Mon-Thu 9:30-6, Fri 9:30-8:30
            Sat 9:30-6:60, Sun 10-4:30

From Tex-Mex ingredients to authentic Mexican cuisine,
QUE PASA offers Vancouver shoppers a spicy shopping

adventure. Prices are competitive and bulk discounts are available.

QUEEN'S PARK MEAT MARKET
402-2ND STREET, NEW WESTMINSTER
PHONE: 521-1622
HOURS: Tue-Fri 8:30-5:30, Sat 8:30- 5

This tiny store is truly a neighbourhood market. Grade "A" No 1 meat and poultry purchased weekly by the master butcher and owner. Meat is hung for least 22 days and is never frozen or cello wrapped. All cuts of meat are available. You can phone in your order and have it delivered if you are in the neighbourhood. New York dressed turkeys available at Thanksgiving and Christmas.

R

RALPH'S FARM PRODUCE
22787 OLD YALE ROAD, LANGLEY
PHONE: 534-4324
HOURS: July-September daily

Features new potatoes (White Warba, Red Norland, Yukon Gold and Yellow Bintje potatoes) and corn (Jubilee Super Sweet and cream corn). Also grows peaches.

RAVENHILL FARM
1330 MOUNT NEWTON CROSSROAD, SAANICH
PHONE: 652-4024   FAX: 544-1185
HOURS: April-August: Sundays 12-5

Culinary herbs, fresh cut and herbs in pots. Happy to offer advice and answer questions about cooking and gardening. Walk through the garden. Completely organic.

RAVENSBERGEN BAKERY SUPPLIES
1600A KINGSWAY, PORT COQUITLAM
PHONE: 942-4656   FAX: 942-8624
HOURS: 8:30-5

Specializes in European ingredients and tools to make desserts like: chocolates, gelato, sorbets, puddings mousses, cakes, pastries and sauces. The company carries only top-of-the-line products. For many items, they have exclusive rights to distribution in Western Canada. Large volume discounts, 99 per cent of business is wholesale. More than 40 years experience in pastry making.

RED CURRANT FARM
34111 SIM ROAD, MATSQUI
PHONE: 826-6521   FAX: 826-6737
HOURS: Daily 8-10

Sells red currants only, available in cardboard flats and plastic pails with 25lb of berries. A small hands-on hobby farm. Will offer discounts on orders over 75lbs, fresh or jam will deliver free as well. Offers U-pick and ready-picked. Uses a minimum of pest and weed sprays.

RENAISSANCE WINE MERCHANTS
33-1035 RICHARDS STREET, VANCOUVER
PHONE: 681-1666   FAX: 687-2959
HOURS: Mon-Fri 8:00-4:30

Do you ever wonder how great Italian restaurants find all those interesting wines that are not available at the LDB? They source them from US. Importers of over 100 of the finest estate-bottled wine of Italy. Sales through LDB and private wine shops, or by the case through Renaissance Wine Merchants. Product and price list available.

REYNELDA FARMS
2194 WESTHAM ISLAND ROAD, LADNER
PHONE: 946-7493

REYNALDA FARMS is a berry oasis situated on Westham Island. Berries are sold ready-picked and U-pick. As well, a variety of jams and other products are available. They specialize in hard-to-find berries and also sell raspberries and strawberries. Once you've finished your berry purchasing, it's just another two minutes to the Reifel Bird Sanctuary, so plan a full day.

RICHARD'S IMPORTED CANDIES
11871 HAMMERSMITH WAY, RICHMOND
PHONE: 274-2626   FAX: 274-2600
HOURS: Mon-Fri 8-5

Specializes in chocolate, cocoa, flavours, dessert cups, mousse mixes, marzipan, decoation, boxed chocolates. A wholesale warehouse and direct importer of some of the world's best dessert ingredients. Callebaut chocolate, chocolate holllow shells for truffle making, cream stabilizers, fruit purees, flavour pastes. Volume sales only. "Chocolate specialists."

RICHMAY FARMS
8928 GIBSON ROAD, CHILLIWACK
PHONE: 795-3029
HOURS: All year: Mon-Sat 8-8.
          Please phone orders ahead.

Sells veal, baby beef and beef. Baby beef is tender and juicy with 10 per cent fat of full size beef. Large volume discounts offered. Full control over every aspect of production.

RICHMOND COUNTRY FARMS
12900 STEVESTON HWY, RICHMOND
PHONE: 274-0522   FAX: 272-5830
HOURS: Winter 9-6, Summer 9-8

Wide range of fruits and vegetables, specializing in local
and Okanagan products. Large volume allows them to
offer unique products, quality and low prices. Large
volume discounts offered in season. Ready picked only.
Very limited spraying through Integrated Pest
Management. Strawberries and blueberries were not
sprayed at all this past season. Home of pumpkin patch
festival, hosting thousands of school children each year.
Occasional special events such as corn roasts, with
music and entertainment.

RICHMOND PUBLIC MARKET
8260 WESTMINSTER HWY, RICHMOND
PHONE: 821-1888
HOURS: Mon-Sat 9:30-7, Sun 9:30-6

Superior Fish Market
Cut Right Meats
Five Seasons Farms
Elite Foods Pine House Bakery
Buy Fresh Gardens
Peppers Produce
Van Den Bosch Patisserie
Antonio's Italian Delicatessen
KRW Turkey Shop
Louisa's Chocolates
Macdonald Poultry

Anatolia Groceries
Riva Gourmet Coffees and Teas
Simply Gourmet
The Coffee Merchants
Richmond Country Chicken
Pacific Housewares
Ephesus Specialty Foods
Grace's Dim Sum and Noodle Shop
Magic Wok
Rainbow Soups and Stocks

ROBSON PUBLIC MARKET
610 ROBSON STREET, VANCOUVER
PHONE: 682-2733   FAX: 682-2776

Adria Delicatessen
Apple Deli
Baba's Baking Company
Bagel Deli
Cookie and Bean Company
Dabne's Food Specialities
Dairy Farm
Divino Wine Shop
Great Canadian Bakery
Hyrise Produce Boutique
Pastameli of New York
RB's Gourmet Butchers
Robson Gourmet Foods
Salmon Shop
Sunburst Natural Vita Foods

RODEAR MEATS
BEAVER VALLEY, WILLIAMS LAKE
PHONE: 922-8207

Canada's first federallly and provincially certified organic
meat-processing plant. Opened in 1990. Meat is sent
weekly to Vancouver in a refrigerated truck. Custom cut.
Used by Chateau Whistler; sold at Capers, and some
family-run food co-ops. In BC's Cariboo country.

ROHAN FARMS
659 McCALLUM ROAD, ABBOTSFORD
PHONE: 852-8060
HOURS   August 29-December 3
            Mon-Fri 11-5:30, Sat 9:30-5:30, Sun 2-5

They feature three varieties of apples: Elstar, Alkemene,
and Jonagold. Also offer unpasteurized apple juice,
homemade apple pies.

RUBINA TANDOORI LAZEEZ CUISINE OF INDIA
1962 KINGSWAY, VANCOUVER
PHONE: 874-3621

An extensive menu, a restaurant that takes you
seriously when you say "Indian hot." Never
disappointing.

RUN-DOWN WALK-UP FARM
9043 184TH STREET, SURREY
PHONE: 882-1278   FAX: 882-2030
HOURS: Daily 9-9

Lambs and honey are sold by this farm. For the last 10 years the lambs have won numerous prizes at the Surrey Fair and the PNE. The stock benefit from excellent pasture management, with rotational grazing. Lambs can be picked up live or custom cutting may be arranged. Will do half-lamb orders whenever possible. No chemical fertilizers are used on the pasture. No growth hormones used.
The honey is made from all the things in the garden: fennel, tomatillos, blackberries, broccoli.

RUSSELL FOOD EQUIPMENT
1255 VENABLES STREET, VANCOUVER
PHONE: 253-6611   FAX: 253-0807
HOURS: Mon-Fri 8-5

This spacious store stocks everything for commercial food service: china, glass, cutlery, all types of pots, cooking utensils, and commercial cooking equipment such as ranges and fryers. High quality products, variety and selection for all budgets. Sale items vary from month to month: phone for details. They offer a variety of quantity discounts. Sell case lots only on selected items. Other outlets across Canada.

S

SABRA'S KOSHER BAKERY AND DELI
3844 OAK STREET, VANCOUVER
PHONE: 733-4912

This wonderful bakery/deli sells typical Middle Eastern fare, with spreads and dips such as babaganouj and tahini, while offering more traditional baked goods that beg to be eaten on the spot. Take their famous walnut roll home and treat yourself to this nutty dessert, or taste one of the poppyseed chocolate pastries from the heaping trays on the counter.

SALMON HOUSE ON THE HILL
2229 FOLKSTONE WAY, WEST VANCOUVER
PHONE: 926-3212
HOURS: Lunch: Mon-Sat 11:30-2:30
        Brunch: Sun from 11:30
        Dinner: Sun-Thu 5-9:30, Fri-Sat 5-10
        Appetizers and Drinks: Daily 2:30-5

Fabulous views. The freshest of seafood and a delightful experience for your taste buds.

SALMON MONTH
PHONE: 926-3212

Call for details.

SALSA, SAMBAS,CHUTNEYS & CHOW CHOWS
C SCHLESINGER & J WILLOUHBY
WILLIAM MORROW & CO, NEW YORK

Exciting recipes for the cook of the nineties.

SANTA FE CAFE
1688 WEST 4TH AVENUE, VANCOUVER
PHONE: 738-8777
HOURS: Dinner: Daily 5:30-10
            Lunch: Mon-Fri 11:30-2:30

Consistently fabulous food.

SEVEN SEAS FISH COMPANY
2344 WEST 4TH AVENUE, VANCOUVER
PHONE: 732-8608   FAX: 732-8342
HOURS: Mon-Sat 9-6

Sells fresh fish from their own boats. No order is too big or small. Other items such as cheese and olives also available. Discounts on bulk orders only and not on sale items.

SHELL ROAD FARM
11411 SHELL ROAD, RICHMOND
PHONE: 241-1943
HOURS: Mid June to early August Mon-Sat 8-Dusk

Sells raspberries, tayberries, gooseberries, limited
number of Transparent and Gravenstein apples and
Bartlett pears. Farm is easily accessible: take Steveston
exit off Highway 99. Pleasant country setting with old
trees, and a good site for your picnic lunch; handout
recipes for fruits given. Discount of 10 per cent for 50lb
or more of berries. Apples and pears ready picked only,
ready and U-pick for raspberries and tayberries. Please
phone ahead to place order. Berries are not sprayed.

SHIMIZU SHOTEN
349 EAST HASTINGS STREET, VANCOUVER
PHONE: 689-3471   FAX: 689-5328
HOURS: Daily 9-7

Specializes in Japanese food, sushi, and pastry. Inside
the modest exterior, has all the hard-to-find Japanese
ingredients, as well as a bakery. Sells fresh and frozen
noodles and green tea ice cream. Bakery items and
sushi are half-price after 6pm.

SIEGLIN ENTERPRISES LTD
33220 HUNTINGDON ROAD, ABBOTSFORD
PHONE: 859-4035
HOURS: June-25-August 6: Mon-Sat 8:30-7

Offers four varieties of ready picked raspberries. Also
sells certified raspberry plants in the spring.
Please phone ahead.

SILVA-GLO TROUT FARMS LTD
7496 272ND STREET, ALDERGROVE
PHONE: 856-2889
HOURS: April to September: Sundays 9-6

U-fish for rainbow trout. Rods and bait provided. Forty acres of forest, farmland, and streams and no fishing licenses are needed. Open to groups throughout the week by prior arrangement.

SILVER BROOK U-CATCH
1364 BRADNER, ALDERGROVE
PHONE: 856-2298

Call for details.

SILVER PALATE COOKBOOK
J ROSSO & S LUKINS
WORKMAN PUB, NEW YORK, 1982

Inspiring and informative.

SINGH FOODS
6684 MAIN STREET, VANCOUVER
PHONE: 327-4911 FAX: 325-8199
HOURS: Daily 9-7:30

Indian spices and groceries, fresh produce. Spice specials offered. Large volume discounts available on case box purchases.

SLAVIC DELICATESSAN
2327 EAST HASTINGS, VANCOUVER
PHONE: 253-1391   FAX: 253-1391
HOURS: Mon-Sat 10-8, Sun 10-6

Specializes in Pirozhki (Perogies), a yeast dough bun
filled with cheddar/potato, sauerkraut/mushrooms,
egg/onion, meat. The best thing about this store is the
guaranteed freshness of the food and the friendly
service. Here you'll find 25 kinds of smoked fish, and 25
kinds of Russian, Ukrainian style chocolates. Very
competitive prices on sausages, and cheeses. 15 per
cent discount on orders of $100 or more.
Catering also available.

SOLLY'S BAGELRY
189 EAST 28TH AVENUE, VANCOUVER
PHONE: 872-1821
HOURS: Tue-Sun 8-6

Traditional hand-rolled, "fat free" bagels. Homemade
vegetarian soups, salads, sandwiches and popular
Jewish pastries. Cinnamon buns, cottage cheese cake,
bagel chips. Fresh frozen bagels, buy six dozen get one
dozen free or six half-dozen for a half-dozen free. Own
cream cheese, lox spread. Organic jams and peanut
butter. Brand new business and response has been
phenomenal.

SONOMA WINE TOUR
PHONE: 280-2801

Call for details.

SOOKE HARBOUR HOUSE
1528 WHIFFEN SPIT ROAD, SOOKE
PHONE: 642-3421

A surreal experience. The ultimate in pampering.

SOUTH CHINA SEAS TRADING COMPANY
1689 JOHNSTON STREET, GRANVILLE ISLAND
PHONE: 681-5402

Prepared items from Asia, Southeast Asia, Africa and
the Caribbean are available. Products with excessive
additives or MSG are not sold. Fresh herbs, including
Thai basil and Kaffir lime leaves, are sold here, as well
as a variety of spices, sauces, condiments, noodles and
rice. Staff is well informed and helpful. Cooking classes
are offered.

SPAGNOL'S SUPER MARKET
602 EWEN AVENUE, NEW WESTMINSTER
PHONE: 228-9816
HOURS: Mon-Sat 8-9, Sun 10-5

Deli platters, instore bakery with many delicious
goodies: cheese sticks, cheese buns and pizzas. Fresh
produce also sold. Their motto is "Big enough to serve,
small enough to care." Features Italian cold cuts and
twice a month a flyer advertises specials. Offers five per
cent discounts to companies and on case lots; 10 per
cent discounts to seniors every Saturday. SPAGNOL'S
has been owned and operated by the same family for
almost 50 years.

SPAGNOL'S WINE AND BEER MAKING SUPPLIES
1325 DERWENT WAY, ANNACIS ISLAND
PHONE: 524-9463   FAX: 524-1327
HOURS: Mon-Fri 8:30-5, Sat 9-5, Sun 10-3

Importers of grapes and grape juice from Washington and California. The company produces wine kits: Cellar classic (45 day kit), Woodbridge Estates (4 weeks), and Cellar Master (4 weeks). Extremely knowledgeable and friendly staff. Every February they have a semi-annual sale where everything is discounted 25 per cent. They also have a Father's Day sale. Case lot discounts on beer malt and wine kits available.

STAR ANISE
1485 WEST 12TH, VANCOUVER
PHONE: 737-1485
HOURS: Lunch: Mon-Fri 11:30-2:30
      Brunch: Sat-Sun 11:30-2:00
      Dinner: Nightly from 5:30

Innovative food and exemplary service.

STARBUCKS
THROUGHOUT THE LOWER MAINLAND

What can be said? Great coffee, wide variety of blends, wonderful graphics and everybody's caffeine fix.

STEVESTON FISH SHOPPE
420 MONCTON, STEVESTON
PHONE: 277-3135   FAX: 277-3181
HOURS: Tues-Sun 10-5

Specializes in bluefin and bigeye tuna, which normally
bypass local stores and are sent directly to Japan.
Excellent smoked salmon also available. Good prices
on other seafood products are a reflection of the boat-to-
shop arrangement that exists when former fishers run
their own retail outlet. Fresh haddock for fish and chips
can be found here, plus products from the Atlantic and
the Caribbean.

STEVESTON PUBLIC FISH SALES FLOAT
STEVESTON PUBLIC MARKET, RICHMOND

Fresh fish and shellfish straight off the boat.

STOCK MARKET
GRANVILLE ISLAND MARKET, VANCOUVER
PHONE: 687-2433

One of the most convenient and inspiring food stores for
the cook, the STOCK MARKET provides the shopper
with demi-glaces, soup stocks, and pestos--to name but
a few essentials. The shop also makes a huge and
changing (seasonal) variety of condiments, dressings,
and sauces that will enliven any meal.

STUBER'S ORCHARD
5384 OLUND ROAD, MT LEHMAN
PHONE: 854-5384
HOURS: August-November (depending on crop)
        Sat, Sun, Holidays 9-4:30

Sells 30 varieties of apples and pears, mostly old-time
varieties no longer available in stores. Sold fresh from
unsprayed trees, at 50 cents a pound. Pest
management done by ducks, chickens, peacocks, and
wild turkeys. This was the first "high-density" orchard in
the Fraser valley, established in 1964 and purchased by
the present owners in 1978. Juice and honey also
available.

SUMAS RIVER FARM
1829 SMITH ROAD RR#2, ABBOTSFORD
PHONE: 859-4231   FAX: 857-1315
HOURS: Mid June-Mid July 9-9

Saskatoon berries, both large and small varieties. Their
fruit is available several weeks earlier than those grown
further east. Both large and small varieties of berries
are available through the harvest season. They are also
sold frozen in 5lb containers or 20lb containers after
harvest while quantities last. Orders over 200 lbs
receive a discount.

SUNSHINE MARKET

3135 OAK STREET, VANCOUVER
PHONE: 738-8623   FAX: 731-9927
HOURS: Daily 10:30-midnight (Open December 25)

Fresh fruits and vegetables; flowers. Attention to quality
of all produce. Chosen as one of the top five for produce
in The Province's "People's Picks." Discounts for large
volumes given depending on product. Family owned
and operated. In the neighbourhood since 1958.

SUPERIOR FISH MARKET

TENANT PARK SQUARE
5229A LADNER TRUNK ROAD, LADNER
PHONE: 946-2097   FAX: 946-4562
HOURS: Mon-Sat 9:30-6
              May-September Open Sundays 11-5

Selling only the freshest fish possible. Salmon caught
from own boats and sold all year round. They package
any fish for air travel and will steak or fillet your fish free
of charge. Their salmon was selected to serve at the
1993 Summit luncheon with Bill Clinton and Boris
Yeltsin. Two specials weekly. Discounts on large orders
(50lb +) of salmon. In business since 1980. Richmond
Public Market, Westminster Hwy, opened in October.
Free recipe booklets. Smoked sockey lox (also
packaged for travel). Specializes also in take home and
heat items, and make your own sushi. Carries a wide
variety of sauces to add while cooking your fish. Prawn,
halibut, cod, sole, snapper, smoked Alaska cod, salt
herring, matjes herring, clams, mussels, oysters,
scallops, double smoked sockeye and much more.

SUR LA TABLE
84 PINE STREET (PIKE MARKET PLACE), SEATTLE
WASH 98101
PHONE: 243-0852
HOURS: Mon-Sat 9-6, Sun 9:30-6

This store has everything a good cook could imagine in
their kitchen...and then some.

SURREY PUBLIC MARKET
6388 KING GEORGE HWY, SURREY
PHONE: 596-8899
HOURS: Daily 9-6:30, Open 'til 8pm Fridays

Rainbow Farm
U-Save Meats
Pasta Please
The Organic Grocer
The Great Canadian Fisherman's Market
The International Bread House
G WIllikers Old Fudge Shop
Pistol and Burnes Coffee House

SUSHI SHOP
ROBSON PUBLIC MARKET
1610 ROBSON STREET, VANCOUVER
PHONE: 682-7280
HOURS: Daily 9-9

A great variety of fresh, healthy and delicious sushi.
Also a list of party platters to choose from. Smoked
salmon rolls, salmon salad rolls, and vegetable maki,

which are difficult to find. Discount coupons given out year round. Party platters require one-day notice.

SWEET CHERUBIM
1105 COMMERCIAL, VANCOUVER
PHONE: 253-0969   FAX: 253-5000
HOURS: Daily 10-8

Specializes in natural foods in bulk and package. Large variety, reasonable prices, volume discounts. Has served Lower Mainland since 1980.

SWEET OBSESSION
2611 WEST 16TH AVENUE, VANCOUVER
PHONE: 739-0555   FAX: 739-0555
HOURS: Tues-Sun 9-10

Cakes and pastries made using all natural ingredients, no mixes, stabilizers or artificial ingredients. Friendly warm atmosphere with emphasis on true quality and each order done to customer's need. Beautiful desserts and pastries which taste sensational. Eat in or take away, coffee and croissants also served.

T

TASTE OF THE NATION
PHONE: 1-202-526-4868
DATE: May 11, 1995

Call for details.

TEN REN TEA & GINSENG COMPANY
550 MAIN, VANCOUVER
PHONE: 684-1566

Sells Chinese teas, such as Jasmine, King's Tea, and Ti Kwan. Offers many varieties of ginseng root, from those grown in the Far East to our own continent. At slower times of business the visitor may participate in a traditional tea ceremony.

TERRA BREADS
2380 WEST 4TH, VANCOUVER
PHONE: 736-1838   FAX: 736-1835

Crusty bread baked on a stone hearth. Uses natural starters for the leavening process. Try the black olive or Italian cheese breads for a unique bread experience, or drop in for a breakfast pastry or one of their excellent Italian sandwiches.

THAI COOKING SCHOOL AT THE ORIENTAL
48 ORIENTAL AVENUE, BANGKOK, THAI 10500
PHONE: 236-0400

Call for a calendar of courses.

THE APPLE FARM
4490 BOUNDARY ROAD, YARROW
PHONE: 823-4311   FAX: 823-4669
HOURS: Daily Aug-Dec 9-6
Weekends Jan-Feb and Apple Blossom
Time (Mid Apr-May)

THE APPLE FARM tries to minimize sprays and uses
no chemical hormones. They feature 22 apple varieties
(grown on 8,000 trees) and nine pear varieties; plums,
crabapples, pumpkins and strawberries.
For a family outing only one hour from Vancouver, THE
APPLE FARM offers a country store, park and petting
zoo. Wholesale (minimum 10 boxes) and box prices
available. Customers can choose from ready picked or
U-pick. The farm uses Integrated Pest Management.
APPLE FARM products also available at Granville
Island Market from September to January on weekends.
The farm hosts an annual Apple Blossom Festival and
also sells fresh, baked, or frozen apple pies, and low-
sugar jams and jellies. Also fresh and pasteurized cider,
dried apples, and different kitchen and gift ideas.

THE BAKEHOUSE BAKERY DELI CAFE
1468 MARINE DRIVE, WEST VANCOUVER
PHONE: 922-3813 FAX: 926-6733
HOURS: Mon-Fri 7-6, Sat 7-5, Sun 10-5

Specializes in providing baked goods for people with
allergies to wheat, yeast, dairy and egg. The bakery
makes breads using spelt, kamut and rice flours, with
and without yeast; also spelt and kamut scones and
muffins. The best thing is the variety. It's a general store
of products organically grown; wheatless cereals, pasta
and grains, 30 types of bread and buns made daily and

173

a deli full of goodies. THE BAKERY has been in this location since the early 1920s.

THE LOBSTER MAN
1807 MAST TOWER (GRANVILLE ISLAND)
PHONE: 687-4288   FAX: 687-5099
HOURS: Daily 9-6

Specializes in live shellfish, products include lobster, crab, mussels, clams, scallops, oysters, geoduck, prawns and smoked salmon. Commitment to quality and friendly service has made THE LOBSTER MAN a seafood tradition on Granville Island for more than 17 years. Carries a large variety of each species of shellfish (10 different types of oysters). Discount prices on quantities larger than 50 pounds. Live shellfish available for your personal selection.

THE NEW BASICS COOKBOOK
J ROSSO & S LUKINS
WORKMAN PUB, 1989

The "Joy of Cooking" of the nineties.

THE PATTY SHOP
4019 MacDONALD, VANCOUVER
PHONE: 738-2144
HOURS: Mon-Sat 9-6:30

Specializes in Jamaican patties: fresh, frozen, cocktail sizes; spicy meat flavours, chicken, vegetables, spinach and cheese and pizza flavours. Top quality product and good prices.

THE PROVINCE
Wednesday edition.

THE REMARKABLE DOG
1735 MARINE, WEST VANCOUVER
PHONE: 922-0334   FAX: 922-0331

Tea is the specialty. Varieties include Chinese Black, Gunpowder Green and Jackson's of Pickadilly rosehip.

THE URBAN GARDENER
BOX 18595 DELTA V4K 4V7
ISABELLE MONTAGNEUX
PHONE: 940-8755   FAX: 940-8755

New publication highlighting the relationship between gardening and food. Recipes included.

THE VANCOUVER SUN

Wednesday edition.

THE VILLAGE BAKER
JOE ORTIZ
TEN SPEED PRESS, CAL, 1993

A treasure for anyone who is serious about baking bread.

THORNCREST FARM
333 GLADWIN ROAD, ABBOTSFORD
PHONE: 853-3108   FAX: 859-6170
HOURS: July 1-March15: Mon-Sat 9-5

Sells gooseberries (red European varieties), red and black currants, sweet corn, apples (Alkmene, Jonagold, Elstar, Fuji, Ida Red), and peaches. Produce can be bought ready-picked or U-pick; even the smallest child can reach the branches of the dwarf apple trees found on the farm. Uses IPM. Recipe sheets for gooseberries given. Pick your own pumpkins beginning October 1. Applefest, featuring orchard tours, apple peeling contests, pumpkin decorating, and a scarecrow decorating contest, held in early fall. Blossomfest, in late April, celebrates the trees in full bloom in springtime. Cider Saturdays start in November and apples, the presses, and the jugs are provided.

TOOLS AND TECHNIQUES
25O 16TH STREET, WEST VANCOUVER
PHONE: 925-1835
HOURS: Mon-Sat 9-6, Fri til 9, Sun 12-5

Sells cookware, dinnerware, linens, barware, glassware, bakeware, cookbooks, cooking utensils, gadgets, gourmet foods, gift baskets, gourmet coffee. Staff is knowledgeable, free gift wrapping offered, bridal registry, cooking school. Special items include Charlotte moulds, paella pans, food colour paste, aspic moulds, spaetzle makers. Celebrating their 10th anniversary this year.

TORREFAZIONE COLIERA
2206 COMMERCIAL DRIVE, VANCOUVER
PHONE: 254-3723
HOURS: Mon-Fri 9:30-6, Sat 9:30-5:30

This coffee store has been in the same location for more than 25 years, and is one of Vancouver's original roasting houses. Specializes in fresh roasted coffee from around the world. Knowledgable staff will guide you through their high quality products to find the blend that will best suit your tastes.

TOSI ITALIAN FOOD IMPORT COMPANY
624 MAIN STREET, VANCOUVER
PHONE: 681 5740   FAX: 685-5704
HOURS: 9:30-6:15

Specializes in Italian products: extra virgin olive oil, pasta, tomatoes, balsamic and wine vinegars, dried tomatoes and mushroom, parmesan and romano cheeses.

TRAIL APPLIANCES
5400 MINORU BOULEVARD, RICHMOND
2550 BARNETT HIGHWAY, COQUITLAM
PHONE: RICHMOND 278-6133FAX : 278-4148
          COQUITLAM 461-1598   FAX: 461-1740
HOURS: Mon-Wed 9-5:30, Thu-Fri 9-9
          Sat 9-5, Sun 12-4

Offers more than 30 different brands of appliances,
built-in, freestanding, North American and European
products. Huge selection; displays show appliances in
kitchen settings, cooking demonstrations, proficient
sales staff and conscientious customer care. Kitchen
ideas and plans can be provided for your kitchen.
Volume discounts available to contractors. Company
founded in Alberta in 1974, and established in BC in
1980.

TRENANT PARK BAKERY AND CAFE
5219 LADNER TRUNK ROAD, LADNER
PHONE: 940-1659   FAX: 271-9828
HOURS: 8-6:30

Baked goods, deli, light lunch items, and catering. Fresh
and affordable. Wholesale prices for restaurant or
companies. Try the delicious pizza; generous slices at
reasonable prices.

TRUE CONFECTIONS
866 DENMAN , VANCOUVER
3701 WEST BROADWAY, VANCOUVER
PHONE: 682-1292   FAX: 682-6158
          BROADWAY: 222-8489
HOURS: Daily 1-midnight, Sat-Sun 1-2am

Desserts, cakes, pies, cheesecakes, wedding cakes,
special occasion cakes. Will cater for desserts only.
Very knowledgable and dedicated staff. Large volume
discounts. All items made in house.

TWO EE'S FARM LTD
16411 FRASER HWY, SURREY
PHONE: 572-1813
HOURS: Summer Mon-Sat 8am-8pm
           Fall and Spring Mon-Sat 8am-7pm
           Winter Mon-Sat 8am-6pm

Sells a wide variety of fruits and vegetables and
delicious honey. Uses IPM. Offers case lot price for
large volume purchases. Business is family-run, started
35 years ago.

TWIN OAKS HERB FARM
4533 232ND STREET, LANGLEY
PHONE: 530-9589

Sells a wide array of herb plants, either potted, fresh cut
in season, or dried. No chemicals or sprays are used.
Fresh vegetables from the garden available as well.

U

UGO AND JOE'S FRESH MEATS AND DELICATESSEN
2404 EAST HASTINGS, VANCOUVER
PHONE: 253-6844
HOURS: Mon-Thu/Sat 8:30-6, Fri 8:30-7:30
       Sun 10-4:30

European groceries, cheeses and cold cuts. Olive oils, pasta, canned tomatoes, homemade Italian sausages and espresso coffee. Carries more than 20 types of olive oil, 12 types of balsamic vinegar. In the neighbourhood for 25 years. Good old fashioned service and great cappuccino. Ugo is the father and Joe is his son. Case lot prices are available to restaurants and businesses receive discount for large volume purchases.

UMBERTO'S PASTA BOOK
UMBERTO MENGHI
DOUGLAS & MCINTYRE, 1985

Who knows pastas better than Umberto?

UPRISING BAKERY
1697 VENABLES STREET, VANCOUVER
PHONE: 254-5635   1-800-818-2299
FAX: 254-6847
HOURS: Mon-Sat 8-6

Whole grain breads, fresh vegetarian soups, salads, sandwiches and full line of morning pastries including muffins, scones, organic croissants and cinnamon buns. High quality ingredients, friendly informed workers who share in the running of the business. Special items: oat fruit cookies (eggless, wheat-free, dairy free, sweetened with brown rice syrup), organic spelt bread for wheat sensitive diets, sourdough pumpernickel is yeast free. Retail and wholesale. Large volume discounts are available on wholesale orders at manager's discretion. Started in 1976, one of Vancouver's "original" natural bakeries. Part of the CRS workers' co-op, a worker owned and operated business with combined net sales more than $15 million per year.

V

VALLEY FRESH FISH
20568B 56TH AVENUE, LANGLEY
PHONE: 534-8717
HOURS: Mon-Thu 10-5;30, Fri-Sat 10-8

Large assortment of freshwater fish, sea fish and shellfish. Large volume discounts at owner's discretion.

VAN CHEONG TEA COMPANY
1050 4151 HAZELBRIDGE WAY, RICHMOND
PHONE: 279-1839

Teas from this company are imported from Taiwan,
from a plantation run by the owner's family. These
award-winning products are also exported to Hong Kong
and Japan. The teas are available in bins or packages,
and are therapeutic: black tea is good for digestion,
ginseng orchid tea helps the eyes and skin; other teas
such as rose and ginseng are also available.

VAN OOSTEROM BERRIES & ORGANIC VEGETABLES
46535 PRAIRIE CENTRAL ROAD, CHILLIWACK
PHONE: 795-9261
HOURS: June-Christmas: Mon-Sat

Sells raspberries, blackberries, gooseberries, endive,
kale, sweet corn, free range eggs. Fresh produce is
sold direct from the yard. Most vegetables are fall
grown, at a time when fresh vegetables are scarce. The
use of crop rotation, green manuring and organic sprays
ensures a chemical-free environment. Please phone
ahead for availability or for orders. Large volume
discounts at certain times, up to 50 per cent.

VANCOUVER COMMUNITY COLLEGE
250 W.PENDER, VANCOUVER
PHONE: 443-8351

Offers great discounts from the school's butcher shop.

VANCOUVER FOOD BANK/FOODRUNNERS
311 EAST 6TH AVENUE VANCOUVER
PHONE: 876-3601   FAX: 876-7323
HOURS: Daily 8:30-5

FOODRUNNERS call themselves the "Robin Hood of the food industry". They deliver prepared and perishable foodstuffs throughout the Lower Mainland. For FOOD BANK drop offs please call: 676-3601.

VANCOUVER MAGAZINE
300 S.E.TOWER 555 WEST 12TH, VANCOUVER
PHONE: 877-7732   FAX: 877-4849

Published 10 times a year. Look for the publications highlighting Vancouver's best food places.

VANCOUVER SPICE COMPANY
BOX 5142, VANCOUVER
PHONE: 530-3247   FAX: 530-4515

This company prides itself on preparing pure spice mixtures of excellent quality and authentic recipes. No MSG or preservatives are added. Although the product is a bit more expensive they strongly recommend that you use it sparingly. Many people with allergies are able to use these mixtures because of their pure quality. Latest products are the Jamaican Jerk Meat Spice and Garam Masala. The latter recipe has been handed down from generations of old family mixtures

VARI BERRY FRUIT DISTRIBUTORS
2644 POINT GREAT ROAD, VANCOUVER
PHONE: 837-8720
HOURS: June-October

Provides farm to fridge service and home fruit delivery
in Vancouver. Fruit includes: raspberries, strawberries,
blueberries, blackberries, gooseberries, red and black
currants. The owner was trained as a chef and has an
excellent knowledge of local products and food services.
Large volume discounts negotiable, depending on
volume.

VENEZIA ICE CREAM
5752 VICTORIA, VANCOUVER
PHONE: 327-8614

The first Italian ice cream parlour in Vancouver, still
keeps busy offering ice cream on Victoria Drive. Twenty
different flavours, such as croccante (rum-nut) and
mango/pineapple.

VILLA DELIA TUSCANY COOKING SCHOOL
1380 HORNBY STREET, VANCOUVER
SCHOOL AT MENGHI'S 54 ACRE VILLA IN TUSCANY
UMBERTO MENGHI
PHONE: 669-3732

Call for details on upcoming courses.

VINTAGE CONSULTANTS
401-611 ALEXANDER STREET, VANCOUVER
PHONE: 251-3366   FAX: 255-3841
HOURS: Mon-Fri 8:30-5

Professional beverage broker and purveyor of fine
wines, spirits and beers, offers free delivery service
throughout the Lower Mainland. Call the "Wine Line"
251-WINE for free expert advice and prompt delivery.
Has access to library wines from leading wineries. Retail
sales at LDB prices only.

W

WEST SIDE SPECIALTY FOODS
1818 WEST 4TH AVENUE, VANCOUVER
PHONE: 737-4338

Fine selection of nuts and seeds, both raw and roasted;
raisins and assorted dried fruits; natural fruit juice
candies; spices, herbs and seasonings; flours, rice,
pasta, peas, beans; soy products; carob products;
Chinese, Japanese and exotic foods: noodles, crackers,
sushi ingredients, hoisin, plum and fish sauces; tofu
cheese, wieners, burgers, and other products.

WESTERN LIVING MAGAZINE
ST 300 SE TOWER 555 WEST 12TH
VANCOUVER   V5Z 4L4
PAULA BROOK
PHONE: 877-7732   FAX: 877-4849

Look for occasional food reviews.

WESTMINSTER QUAY PUBLIC MARKET
810 QUAYSIDE,   NEW WESTMINSTER
PHONE: 520-3881
HOURS: Daily 9:30-6:30, Fri until 8pm

Akira Sushi
Alpine Bakery
Cheese Please
Croissant Chalet
Daily Catch Seafood
Farm Cottage Bakery
Fraser's Riverside Deli
Fresh Choice Meats
Johnston Farms
Key West Pasta
New West Farms
Pastameli
Quay Quality Turkey
Savoury Salmon
Sue's Cottage Kitchen
Sweet 'n' Natural
Tout Sweet

WILLOWVIEW FARMS
288 McCALLUM RD (EXIT #90), ABBOTSFORD
PHONE: 854-8710
HOURS: July-Christmas: Mon-Sat 9-6
Christmas-April 30: Wed-Sat 9-6

Crops sold: apples, kotata blackberries, rhubarb, dwarf apple trees, pumpkins, and Saskatoon berries (1996). Crops are picked at the peak of ripeness and freshness is maintained by rapid cooling in refrigerated storage. Retail and wholesale prices are offered. Ready picked produce only. Farm uses IPM. Family farm established in 1960.

WINDEMERE NUT GROVE
50131 CAMP RIVER ROAD, CHILLIWACK
PHONE: 794-7139
HOURS: Mon-Sat all year round

Wonderful hazelnuts.

WINE TIDINGS
KYLIX MEDIA INC, Suite 414, 5165 Sherbrooke Street West, Montreal, Quebec, H4A 1T6
(514) 481-6606 or 481-6606

An informative wine and food magazine published eight times a year.

WISEBEY VEGGIES
FARMSTAND: 40236 NO 3 ROAD
FARM HOME: 3185 TOLMIE ROAD, YARROW
PHONE: 823-4617
HOURS: June-November: Daily 9-6
          December-May: Fri-Sun 10-4

Almost every kind of produce can be found here, from potatoes and peas to herbs, pickling cucumbers, and pumpkins. U-Pick or ready pick. The Wisebey's also sell local berries, honey, jams, and ornamental grasses.

WINE AND DINE

For information on this festival please call: 926-6339

Y

YELLOW POINT LODGE
RR3, LADYSMITH, BC
PHONE: 245-7422

A peaceful retreat with excellent West Coast cuisine.

YOKA'S COFFEE AND HONEY
3171 WEST BROADWAY, VANCOUVER
PHONE: 738-0905   FAX: 731-0097
HOURS: Mon-Sat 9-6, Sun 10-5

Arabian coffees roasted on premises; bulk teas; BC honey; quality hand grinders and espresso makers. Also sells, zisha Chinese tea pots and brass Turkish mills that can be used to grind pepper. Large volume discounts offered. They use a 1930s nickel-plated roasting machine.

Z

ZORBA'S BAKERY & FOODS LTD
7173 BULLER AVENUE, BURNABY
PHONE: 439-7731   FAX : 439-0525
HOURS: Mon-Fri 7:30-5

This outlet offers pita bread, homous, tzatziki, and other Greek specialties at wholesale prices.
No additives used. ZORBA'S also makes peanut butter.

Caralyn Campbell is a full-time advertising feature writer for Pacific Press. She has two children, two cats and a dog, bakes weekly orders of bread for friends and neighbours, caters the occasional dinner party and in her spare time, she breathes deeply into a paper bag.

Tracey Shelley-Lavery is a teacher who loves to cook and bake. She attributes her fondness for classical music and fine ingredients to her grandmas Polly and Annie. Tracey's motto is: "eat some chocolate, you'll feel better."

For ordering information , and volume discount quotes contact Dog Eared Books at 943-2399, or write to them at

DOG EARED BOOKS
1628 FARRELL CRESCENT
DELTA, BC
V4L 1V1